Arthur Miller's

THE CRUCIBLE

AND
A MEMORY OF
TWO MONDAYS
A VIEW FROM THE BRIDGE
AFTER THE FALL
INCIDENT AT VICHY

JOAN THELLUSSON NOURSE
DEPARTMENT OF ENGLISH
ST. JOHN'S UNIVERSITY

MONARCH
PRESS

Published by
MONARCH PRESS
a Simon & Schuster division of
Gulf & Western Corporation
Simon & Schuster Building
1230 Avenue of the Americas
New York, N.Y. 10020

MONARCH PRESS and colophon are trademarks of Simon & Schuster, registered in the U.S. Patent and Trademark Office.

Standard Book Number: 0-671-00687-8

Library of Congress Catalog Card Number: 66-1892

Printed in the United States of America

CONTENTS

INTRODUCTION

MILLER AND *THE CRUCIBLE*. On January 22, 1953, *The Crucible* opened in New York at the Martin Beck theatre. This was the fifth Broadway offering by Arthur Miller, then but thirty-seven years old. Both the public and the critics had come to expect a great deal from the young playwright whose *Death of a Salesman,* some four years earlier, had received the Pulitzer Prize and many other coveted awards. Reactions to *The Crucible,* however, were not altogether favorable. Ostensibly it was a historical play dealing with the witchcraft trials that occurred in seventeenth-century Massachusetts. Yet it seemed also to have contemporary political implications, and some regarded it as a noble effort to demand in our time greater respect for the rights of individuals. On the other hand, some who had been much impressed with the technical virtuosity of *Death of a Salesman,* found *The Crucible* a disappointing return to more conventional treatments. In addition, they deplored what seemed to them a slow-moving, rather diffuse first act.

CHANGING ATTITUDES. Because of this lukewarm reception, the play ran for only six months, closing in July of the same year; whereas *Death of a Salesman* had been performed 742 times, running for over a year and a half. Subsequently, however, the Salem drama was revised both on and off Broadway and was often on the performance schedule of colleges and little theatre groups. At present its reputation is high. It is no longer so much the subject of heated controversy, since the government investigations it seemed to criticize are no longer headline news. But its solid merits strictly as drama have been increasingly recognized. It is a powerful work, with exciting conflicts, strong suspense, and interesting, admirable characters. Moreover, the dialogue, with its colorful terms from our colonial past, has about it a vigorous, sinewy eloquence. Above all, there is here the passionate expression of an idealism that is characteristically American.

MILLER'S CRAFTSMANSHIP. Most critics today would agree that Arthur Miller's technical proficiency is of a high order. From the time he entered the University of Michigan in the mid-thirties, he has studied and practiced his craft. Actually he won several prizes for playwriting at the University and later wrote radio scripts in New York. He especially admired Henrik Ibsen, the great Norwegian master of the "well-made" or tightly constructed play; but he also was familiar with the work of O'Neill, Odets, and Wilder, as well as that of such European experimentalists as Brecht. *All My Sons* (1947), the first of his dramas to receive general acclaim, seemed largely to follow the Ibsen tradition. *Death of a Salesman,* however, two years later, handled its material more freely, cleverly using flashbacks to permit startling insights into

5

its hero's psychology. *The Crucible* had a different approach, since to the playwright, the over-all political issues were at least as important as the inner workings of any one character's mind. Hence, Miller used a long, expository first scene as "overture," to acquaint his audiences as thoroughly as possible with the tense situation in Salem. Later, in *After the Fall*, he would again use flashbacks, this time even more extensively than in *Death of a Salesman*, to reveal how a man's thinking is influenced by his past. Actually, the one important fact about Miller's style as a dramatist is that he is continually varying it to achieve different effects. So those who expect any new work to follow the course set by the previous one are almost always disappointed. Certain of his experiments, of course, are more successful than others. But he has at least consistently demonstrated an enterprising and progressive approach to his craft.

MODERN TRAGIC DRAMAS. If Miller is noted for stimulating experiments with technique, he has also been widely discussed as a writer of modern tragedies. In earlier ages, tragic plays had dealt mainly with the overthrow of such powerful figures as kings or generals. Miller, however, has argued that an ordinary modern individual can serve equally well as tragic hero, if he wants something intensely enough to give up everything else in its pursuit. Actually, he need not be thoroughly clear as to his goals— Miller's tragic figures are often somewhat confused. Yet if there is something decent about what he desires so passionately, he can still be regarded as making a truly tragic commitment.

For example, in *Death of a Salesman*, which is discussed in more detail in another *Monarch Review Notes and Study Guide*, Willy Loman is not clear at all in his thinking about success and happiness and the obligations of parent and child. He gives his sons Biff and Happy unrealistic counsel as to how to achieve happiness; and his eventual suicide to get the insurance money for Biff is a highly questionable solution to the family's problems. Yet, essentially, Willy is a father who wants to provide well for his sons and leave them a splendid heritage. As an over-all objective this is not by any means contemptible. And, according to the Miller theory, there is a recognizable tragic stature even in a poor, distracted, unimpressive salesman, if he is willing to give his life for his convictions.

Somewhat similar patterns are apparent in other Miller plays. Ed Keller in *All My Sons* puts the interests of his household above all else, and lets the defective plane parts be shipped out from his factory rather than jeopardize the family business. When, however, his son Chris rejects him, he can no longer see any reason to live, and kills himself. Again, in *A View from the*

Bridge, Eddie Carbone, a longshoreman, does not want his young niece to marry a light-hearted immigrant, Rodolpho. Actually, Eddie has subconscious feelings of jealousy that make him regard the young man with unreasonable hostility. Yet Eddie in his own way means well, and the drastic step he eventually takes to prevent the marriage costs him his own life.

In *The Crucible,* John Proctor, the blunt, sensible farmer, is not so obviously guilty of any such obsession. Yet he, too, is a common man, rather than a traditional influential leader. He is by no means overly anxious to engage in any heroic action. In fact, he tends to be cautious, and even seriously considers confessing to a lie to save his life. Yet in the long run, he cannot sign a statement that he regards as shamefully false. So he goes to his death, his self-respect intact. And many who have hesitated about admitting the tragic stature of such muddled individuals as Willy and Eddie have been more than willing at least to concede it to sturdy, responsible John Proctor.

MILLER AND THE SOCIAL DRAMA. In addition to being classified as "psychological dramas" and "modern tragedies," Arthur Miller's works are sometimes listed as "social dramas." This last category refers to plays that deal with issues affecting contemporary society. Eugene O'Neill, John Steinbeck, and Clifford Odets were among the American playwrights before Miller who had taken up various social questions. And Miller's early master, Ibsen, had done much to establish the genre many years before.

In *All My Sons,* Miller had considered the matter of public responsibility. Ed Keller is a reasonably good American family man, who has even lost a son in the war. But Keller will send out defective products to the Army rather than lose contracts that may destroy his business. He has a normally creditable ambition to leave something valuable to his surviving son, Chris. But Chris —and obviously Miller—insists that as a man Keller has no right to destroy the sons of others to protect the material interests of his own. In developing this situation, Miller is clearly indicting all those Americans who take advantage of a national crisis to turn everything to their own selfish profit.

In *Death of a Salesman,* there are other aspects of American life that Miller views with suspicion. He objects to the callous, inhumane attitude of a business world, so competitive that it will lack all consideration for workers as individuals. He also criticizes his countrymen's overemphasis upon material success, and their overstressing of superficial personality traits to the detriment of solid character building.

The Crucible, and such later works as *After the Fall* and *Incident at Vichy,* take up again, in more universal terms, the question of social responsibility. Obviously some of those who are supporting the witchcraft persecutions have strictly personal objectives in view. Abigail wants her mean revenge, Putnam wants more land, and the judges want to escape being accused of having acted unjustly. Yet all are shirking their responsibilities as human beings. In addition, John Proctor, when considering the possibility of making a false confession, knows that in so doing he will be betraying his friends to some extent. Proctor, however, is a responsible man, and eventually does the right thing.

Again in *After the Fall,* Quentin does much thinking about the matter of betrayal, of putting the self above others to whom one owes obligations. And although he personally would never willingly have supported the terrible Nazi persecutions, he wonders, as does Holga, whether anyone who escaped death in them had not in some way been partially guilty. This idea is developed further in *Incident at Vichy,* Miller's most recent play, about ten men arrested by the Nazis, who will execute them if they prove to be Jewish. In this work, the prince indicates that he has always viewed the Nazis with loathing and contempt, and has even fled his homeland, because they have contaminated it. But the doctor argues that unless one actively opposes an evil, he is failing in his human responsibility. Of course, once more, Miller is not talking merely of his two characters in a type of situation that existed a generation ago. As a writer of dramas of social criticism, he is advocating that all men accept their obligation to combat continually whatever evils threaten their civilization, even at the sacrifice of immediate personal interests.

EARLY YEARS. Born in New York City on October 17, 1915, Arthur Miller was the son of an Austrian-born clothing manufacturer. He grew up in Brooklyn, which he would use as the setting for *Death of a Salesman* and *A View from the Bridge.* In both plays he notes changes occurring during those years. Willy Loman, for instance, saw the almost rural area of small houses with flower and vegetable gardens yield to tall apartment buildings. And Alfieri, the lawyer in the later work, saw its waterfront become more "civilized." Although Miller says little directly about his home life, there are at least autobiographical hints in his plays. The genial side of Joe Keller may well have been suggested by his father's good-natured joking; and *After the Fall* indicates that his mother gave early encouragement to his literary promise.

DEPRESSION YEARS. Graduating from Brooklyn's Abraham Lincoln High School in 1932, Miller hoped to go to college, but the Depression had limited family finances. Several of his works reflect how hard men had to work to make a living during those years. Eddie, in *A View from the Bridge,* tells of the struggle to support his family; and it is clear that both Ed Keller and Willy Loman never found it very easy to forge ahead. In any event, to earn money toward a higher education, young Miller worked for two years in a warehouse supplying automobile parts. Certain of the more pleasant aspects of this experience he recalls in his short play, *A Memory of Two Mondays.* Subsequently he was able to go on to the University of Michigan. There he won the Avery Hopwood Award for his first play, *The Grass Still Grows.* He went on then to write other dramas, completing his college course by means of a part-time newspaper job and help from the National Youth Administration.

RECOGNITION IN NEW YORK. Returning east after his 1938 graduation, Miller continued to create plays, while holding various posts to make a living. He is said to have worked in a box factory and the Navy Yard, to have driven a truck, waited on tables, and served as crew-man on a tanker. He also was connected with the Federal Theatre Project, wrote radio scripts, and did research for a film. In 1944 he brought out a war commentary, *Situation Normal,* and in the following year he published a novel against anti-Semitism, called *Focus.* His first play to receive a Broadway hearing, as indicated previously, was *The Man Who Had All the Luck* (1944). But full-scale success was attained actually with *All My Sons* (1947) and *Death of a Salesman* (1949).

AMERICAN FAMILY TRAGEDIES. Both *All My Sons* and *Death of a Salesman* deal with the business and domestic problems of middle-class American families. Both concern a father in conflict with two sons whose love and respect he ardently desires. Ed Keller wants, above all, to leave his boys a thriving business. But one, Larry, dies in the war. The other, Chris, is appalled to learn that while he was fighting overseas, his father shipped out defective plane parts. Rejected and condemned by his surviving son, Keller commits suicide. Never so prosperous as Ed Keller, Willy Loman too has great hopes for his sons, especially the elder, Biff. Willy brags to both of his being well-liked, and assures them of a great future awaiting them. Biff, disillusioned upon discovering his father's deceptions, drifts from job to job, while Happy resentfully makes up for his insignificant position by sensual self-indulgence. Unable to accept their failure and his own, Willy kills himself so that he can at least leave some impressive insurance money.

Of the two, *All My Sons* is the more conventional in form, with *Death of a Salesman* achieving fluidity by the skilled use of flashbacks. In both, the heroes are not highly intelligent and are not given to much genuinely perceptive self-criticism. They mean well, in general, but having accepted certain values uncritically, find it hard to see where they went wrong. In both instances their sons come to reject their standards and angrily point out why. This means heartbreak for the older men, with Keller seeing more of the light than Willy ever does. Dramatically there is more good lively conflict in such father-son scenes; and through the opposed points of view Miller is able to make some telling comments upon the twentieth-century American scene.

THE SALEM CHALLENGE. In 1950, Miller paid tribute to Ibsen, whose work he admired, by adapting the latter's fiery play about a repudiated idealist, *An Enemy of the People.* This, however, closed after a short run, although several years later it enjoyed some success off-Broadway. In 1953 Miller offered a new original work, *The Crucible,* based upon the trials for witchcraft that occurred in Massachusetts in the 1690's. In our own time the term "witch hunt" was sometimes used to describe contemptuously various investigations launched by Congressional and other groups to expose un-American activities. Since it was understood that Miller himself had little sympathy for such official inquiries, many sought to reduce his play to a simple allegory. Actually it is no mere propaganda piece, although certainly there is, by implication, criticism of the attitudes and methods of some later interrogators. Subsequently Miller himself was to be called before a Congressional Committee and convicted for failing to cite the names of those formerly known to have engaged in radical activities. And his 1963 drama *After the Fall* would have more to say regarding such political probes.

The Crucible tells of the havoc wrought in early Salem when some restless young girls claim that witches are abroad in the village. Their leader, the beautiful and vindictive Abigail Williams, hopes for revenge against Elizabeth Proctor, from whose service she was dismissed after having had an affair with Elizabeth's husband, John. As more accusations are made, and many, including Elizabeth, arrested, John Proctor joins with other sensible townsmen to stop the outrages. Charged himself and imprisoned, he must decide whether to live and make a living for his children even if this means swearing to a vicious lie, or going to his death rather than deny the truth. He makes the second choice. Like Ed Keller and Willy Loman, he thus makes a full commitment, but sees issues more clearly, his sacrifice thus appearing more meaningful. A noteworthy feature of this drama is the language used to suggest the blunt but forceful idiom of the early colonists.

TWO SHORT PLAYS. Two and a half years later, in September, 1955, Miller offered a double bill of two short works, neither of which was particularly well received. The first, *A Memory of Two Mondays*, was a brief mood piece, based upon his youthful experiences in the auto-parts warehouse. The young office boy, Bert, who takes the job, as did Miller, to earn money for college, manifests a friendly interest in the joys and sorrows of fellow-employees, while wondering how they go on seemingly content with routine work over the years. When he leaves, however, he is saddened to realize how readily they will forget him. Snatches of poetry and certain softening effects in set and lighting cast an almost romantic glow over mundane happenings in the drab, dingy old factory.

As for *A View from the Bridge,* here Miller chose to deal with Brooklyn residents quite different culturally from those in *Death of a Salesman.* Again, however, the tone was tragic, and conflict was developed between family members of two generations. Again the father figure would seek blindly to safeguard the future for the young, and again be rejected and go to his death violently. Eddie Carbone, a hard-working longshoreman, is overly fond of his wife's niece, Catherine. When the girl falls in love with Rodolpho, an illegal immigrant sheltered by the Carbone family, Eddie convinces himself that the marriage would not be a good one for Catherine. Unable to dissuade her, he eventually turns informer and dies in a knife duel with Rodolpho's irate brother. Like Willy Loman, Eddie is not overly intelligent and cannot perceive his bias even when enlightened by the wise lawyer, Alfieri. But once certain that his course is right, Eddie, too, gives full commitment. So he is another unyielding Miller hero, willing to give up everything for his tenaciously held belief. An interesting departure in this work is the use of the cultivated Alfieri as chorus, suggesting interpretations that could not be formulated by Eddie's uneducated group. And some critics have indicated other echoes in this play of older tragic themes. Yet, this too is a play about a "common man," passionately determined and uncompromising. Dissatisfied with the work's original form, Miller later expanded the piece to a full-length play. Revived off-Broadway during the 1964-1965 season, this longer form was now hailed with enthusiasm as a strong, effective tragic drama.

AFTER THE FALL. No new plays by Miller appeared during the next nine years, until *After the Fall* opened at the new American National Theatre and Academy (ANTA) theatre in New York in 1964. During that time, however, significant events occurred in Miller's life. In 1956 and 1957, for instance, he was summoned before Congressional committees and found guilty of contempt of Congress. This conviction was later reversed. Also during this period were marital difficulties. After a divorce from his first wife, Mary Slattery, by whom he had two children, he married in 1956 the well-known motion-picture star, Marilyn Monroe. With her in mind, he wrote a poignant story, *The Misfits,* and adapted it for the screen. She starred in the film with Clark Gable. But this union, too, ended in divorce, and he subsequently wed a young European woman, Ingeborg Morath.

Like *Death of a Salesman, After the Fall* uses flashbacks to show what memories affect a man's thinking, but here all action takes place in the head of its hero, the lawyer, Quentin. There are no "outside" scenes, such as those between Linda and the boys, which are hardly in Willy Loman's thoughts. The setting is colorless and almost abstract. And characters appear and vanish readily as Quentin thinks about them. In general, Quentin, twice divorced and considering a third marriage to a German girl, reviews his life to date. He recalls unhappy scenes with his first wife, Louise. He painfully relives episodes occurring at the time old friends were summoned before Congressional committees. And above all, he keeps adverting to his turbulent second marriage to an unstable blonde entertainer, Maggie, who later died a suicide. Agonizing over the problem of guilt, his own and that of others typified in Nazi atrocities, he finally takes heart from the counsels of Holga, the German girl, to accept his limitations and go on with courage and hope. The autobiographical element in this work attracted considerable attention. In particular, the rather sensational scenes with Maggie, the self-deceiving singer lost through drink and drugs, gave rise to comment. Some thought the apparent revelations in poor taste; others merely found the episodes intensely dramatic. The over-all format, too, was the subject of controversy, some finding it too diffuse for any satisfactory development of plot or characters. Incidentally, Maggie's false image of herself recalls the instances of self-deception in *All My Sons, Death of a Salesman,* and *A View from the Bridge.* And the scenes of family conflict from Quentin's boyhood recall the bitter domestic quarrels in earlier works.

INCIDENT AT VICHY. Also produced in 1964, this somewhat shorter work deals more fully with the question of Nazi crimes raised in *After the Fall.* In 1942, ten men, suspected of being Jewish, are brought in for questioning in Vichy, France. As the play proceeds, the ten prisoners speculate fearfully as to their fate, hopefully exploring every suggestion that all may yet be well. The final debate is begun by an intense Jewish psychiatrist who tries to convince an Austrian Catholic prince, arrested in error, that all who do not actively oppose the persecution of others are partially responsible for the resultant horrors. Appalled at this accusation, the prince gives his own pass to freedom to the doctor, thus accepting responsibility. Audiences in general seem to find this work a moving experience. The stakes are high, the suspense is continual, and the discussions are lively and revealing. Also interesting is the fact that with no intermission the action could realistically take place in the time allotted for the play. Adverse critics, however, have found little that is new said about the World War II atrocities, and have found ten "typical" characters little more than personifications of certain points of view.

SUMMATION. During the twenty years following his first Broadway production in 1944, Arthur Miller has remained in the forefront of important American playwrights. Most anthologies and histories of the drama in this country give space to his works, and productions of his works have been given overseas. He has, of course, not escaped adverse criticism. His language has been called banal and lacking in emotional power. He has been attacked as too negative in his view of American society and especially as unfair to American business. Again there have been those who have rejected his concept of tragedy as meanly bourgeois, regarding his "common man" heroes as "little" and "common" in the worst sense, or not genuinely human enough to qualify as tragic figures at all. Nor have his technical approaches been universally approved. *All My Sons* was found to be too rigidly constructed, and *After the Fall* too diffusely constructed. The Act One "Overture" to *The Crucible* has annoyed some commentators, and the terminal "Requiem" to *Death of a Salesman* has annoyed others.

Yet the very prevalence of so much controversy over this dramatist testifies to his influential position in the American theatre. Regardless of objections posed to this or that individual aspect of his work, he retains an essentially unchallenged reputation. And even those who take issue with him have found admirable his continuing efforts to devise suitable new forms to express new and different themes. Even among those who disagree with his literary, political and social views are many who still find him a stimulating writer, one who at least does do some thinking about vital contemporary issues. Finally, audiences for two decades have found his plays good theatre. They have wept over the death of poor, battered old Willy Loman, and have been awed by the plain-spoken, solid integrity of John Proctor. They have watched fascinated as deluded Eddie baits Rodolpho, they have listened with shock to the tirades of the embittered Maggie, and they have sympathized warmly with the diffidently heroic Austrian prince. Whatever else may be said, Miller commands the attention and stirs the hearts of most who come to see his dramas. And this gift is what most conclusively labels him a major playwright.

THE CRUCIBLE

(1953)

CHARACTERS

REVEREND PARRIS. Small-minded, irascible minister of Salem—unpopular with many—who loudly decries witchcraft, being very conscious that his own household is not above suspicion.

BETTY PARRIS. His motherless ten-year-old daughter, whose strange malady causes Salem to wonder if diabolical forces are at work.

TITUBA. The minister's Negro slave, brought from Barbados, who leads strange rites in the forest and will confess whatever those in power seem most disposed to pardon.

ABIGAIL WILLIAMS. Parris's teen-aged niece, formidable leader of the young accusers, previously seduced by John Proctor while living on his farm as servant to his wife.

SUSANNA WALCOTT. A younger member of Abigail's band, a breathless, apprehensive girl.

MRS. ANN PUTNAM. A morbid, disturbed woman of forty-five, convinced that some evil spirit destroyed her babies at birth.

THOMAS PUTNAM. Her aggrieved, wealthy husband, bitterly determined to pay back his enemies and to acquire more and more land.

MERCY LEWIS. His plump eighteen-year-old servant, a cruel and crafty disciple of Abigail.

MARY WARREN. The timid, wavering current maid at the Proctors', essentially decent but easily confused and terrified of Abigail.

JOHN PROCTOR. Blunt, sensible farmer, hostile to Parris and his cry of witchcraft, but appalled to think that his guilty affair may impel Abigail to destroy his wife.

REBECCA NURSE. Widely respected, aged pillar of the community, fantastically charged with devil-worship, apparently because the Putnam clan recalled spitefully certain boundary disputes with her family.

GILES COREY. A brave, honest, but contentious farmer in his eighties, always in and out of lawsuits, who pays dearly for a foolish comment upon his wife's fondness for books.

14

REVEREND JOHN HALE. An earnest, scholarly, young theologian, intent upon restoring peace and order in Salem by using his knowledge, but distressed to find fanaticism rampant.

ELIZABETH PROCTOR. The conscientious, rather inflexible wife of John Proctor, hurt by his infidelity and finding it hard to understand and forgive.

FRANCIS NURSE. A much-revered older man, the loyal husband of Rebecca, who joins with Proctor and Corey in a valiant effort to prove the innocence of their unjustly accused wives.

EZECHIEL CHEEVER. A blustery but uncertain court official, who serves warrants and dutifully recalls damaging statements made by men like Proctor in opposing the mass arrests.

MARSHAL HERRICK. Another official of the court, in his thirties, a compassionate man, who regretfully obeys the laws and takes Elizabeth and the others off to jail.

JUDGE HAWTHORNE. A hard, merciless old Salem judge, coldly certain that those trying to defend accused witches must be part of a plot to undermine the authority of the court.

DEPUTY GOVERNOR DANFORTH. Another elder spokesman for justice, more humane in manner than Hawthorne but equally strict in quelling all opposition.

SARAH GOOD. An old Salem woman, ragged and confused, who confesses promptly when accused and thereafter shares wild visions with Tituba in the jail.

HOPKINS. A guard at the Salem jail.

SETTING

The action occurs in and around Salem in the year 1692. The first act takes place in a small upstairs bedroom in the house of Parris, the minister. The second act takes place in the common room of John Proctor's farm home, the third in the vestry room of the meeting house, and the fourth in a cell of the jail.

Note: The printed text of the play includes an introduction and comments on the characters and events. In some productions these are delivered by an onstage narrator. In others they are omitted.

PLOT ANALYSIS

ACT I (AN OVERTURE). In the spring of 1692, Reverend Samuel Parris, the petty, irritable minister of Salem, Massachusetts, is worried about his small daughter, Betty. She has slept, seemingly in a trance, since he caught her with his teen-aged niece, Abigail, and other girls dancing in the forest the night before. With them was his Barbados slave, Tituba, but Abigail denies that there was any Devil-worship or conjuring. Someone already has summoned the Reverend John Hale, a witchcraft specialist from nearby Beverly. But Abigail insists that she is virtuous, even though she was lately discharged as servant by John Proctor's wife. The latter, she claims, is a spiteful liar.

Thomas Putnam, a shrewd, ruthless landowner, arrives with Ann, his gloomy, neurotic wife. Their daughter, too, is sick, and Mrs. Putnam is certain that witchcraft is abroad. Why else would she have lost so many babies, all dying soon after birth? Parris disputes her theory since his own niece and daughter took part in the now admitted conjuring. But Mary Warren, the Proctors' present servant, enters to announce excitedly that talk of witches is all over Salem. Left alone briefly with Abigail, the girls, including Mary, the awakened Betty, and Mercy Lewis, the Putnams' crafty maid, worry about how much more they should admit. Abby, however, warns them to say no more or she will make them pay dearly.

John Proctor, a vigorous, independent farmer, enters and irately orders home his servant, Mary, who leaves followed by Mercy. John jests briefly about the scare with Abigail, with whom he has had an affair. He firmly denies, however, that he still loves her, and is angered by her vindictive references to his wife. At this point a psalm is heard sung by villagers, Betty starts screaming, and Parris and the Putnams return.

Also arriving now are two elderly personages—cantankerous Giles Corey and gentle, dignified Rebecca Nurse. Rebecca easily soothes the agitated child. She antagonizes the Putnams, however, who have often been at odds with her family, by her common-sense refusal to get overly exercised over a youngster's hysteria. Rebecca has had twenty-six grandchildren! A quarrel then breaks out between Proctor, lining up with Rebecca, and the Putnams, intent upon proving diabolical influence. It is also evident that Proctor dislikes the fiery sermons and mean avarice of the Reverend Mr. Parris. In addition, Proctor and Corey rouse Putnam's ire further by claiming lumber that he says belongs to him.

Arriving with several weighty books, the Reverend John Hale

energetically proposes to sift the whole witchcraft question. Sure of himself and of his learning, he listens attentively to the Putnams and even to crotchety old Corey's suspicions that his wife, Martha, reads too much. Hale is appalled to learn of the forest rites and sends for Tituba. Terrified for her life, the slave heeds the minister's leading questions and confesses with imaginative gusto. Pressed to name witches, she cooperatively accuses two questionable old women, Sarah Good and Sarah Osburn. The bystanders are impressed. And Abigail, exalted and aglow, also piously confesses, adding more names, as does the feverish Betty. Putnam, triumphant, goes to call the marshal to arrest those listed and to put them in chains. Parris prays thankfully.

ACT II. One night a week later, at Proctor's farm, John talks with his wife, Elizabeth. She tries to be dutiful and even agreeable, but clearly cannot forget his infidelity. Proctor is alarmed to learn that many have been arrested in Salem, that notable judges have come, and that there is talk of hangings. Elizabeth urges him to denounce the formidable Abigail. When he hesitates, she eyes him accusingly, and he, in turn, rebukes her for being cold and unforgiving.

Timorous Mary Warren, now a lofty court official, enters, giving Elizabeth a hand-made poppet, or rag doll. Obviously horrified and sick, Mary tells them that Goody Osburn is set to hang, Sarah Good having saved herself by confessing. She adds that Elizabeth herself was mentioned, but that she loyally came to her defense. Proctor's wife now knows that Abigail seeks her life. John is incredulous, but agrees now to go and testify that Abigail admitted the fraud to him.

Suddenly Hale appears, to do some investigating on his own initiative. He notes Proctor's limited church attendance, refusing to grant that disliking Parris is any valid excuse. Challenged to repeat the Ten Commandments, John ironically forgets the one against adultery. At Elizabeth's prodding, he tells Hale of Abigail's falsehoods. As for himself, he cautiously avoids rejecting the possibility of witches. But Elizabeth firmly declares that if she can be accused, then there are no real witches.

Corey and Nurse arrive, angry and disturbed, to report the arrest of their wives. Even Hale is shocked to hear Rebecca charged with supernaturally slaying the Putnam infants. Two court officials, Cheever and Herrick, then come to take Elizabeth, whom Abigail has finally charged. Mary's doll is urged as evidence, for a needle stuck in the doll could be a witch's way of inflicting stabbing pains in her victim. The story is largely disproved, but despite John's outraged objections, his wife is taken and chained. Hale

promises to plead for her, however, and John warns the petrified
Mary to tell the truth and save her mistress.

ACT III. In the meeting-house vestry room, now a court ante-
chamber, Corey, noisy and contentious, is barred from offering
evidence to save his wife. Stern Judges Hawthorne and Danforth
accuse him of trying to undermine the court. Corey, Nurse, and
Proctor then bring in the frightened Mary Warren to declare all
the girls liars.

Questioning Proctor closely, the suave Danforth assures him that
he need not try this to save Elizabeth. She claims to be an ex-
pectant mother and will not be executed for some time. Proctor,
however, will not desert his friends. The men present an affidavit,
with over ninety signatures, asserting the high opinion held by
neighbors of all the accused wives. They are shocked, however,
to hear that all those loyal friends will be hauled into court. Corey,
in turn, charges Putnam with backing the accusations to gain
lands. Unable, in conscience, to name his source for this charge,
Corey is arrested for contempt.

Mary then fearfully testifies, and the girls are brought in to con-
front her. Abigail coolly accuses her of lying. As a test, the judges
order Mary to faint as she did in court, but Mary cannot oblige.
Unable to rouse interest enough in the forest revels, Proctor desperately admits his adultery to discredit Abigail. He adds that
his wife, who never lies, will support his contention. Hastily
summoned, Elizabeth charitably shields his good name, thus
unintentionally blasting his case. Emboldened, Abigail leads her
set in a wild, frenzied outburst to frighten the wits out of Mary.
Weakening, the quavering girl rejoins the rest and accuses Proctor.
Hale tries to intercede for him, but the judges send Proctor and
Corey to prison.

ACT IV. In the Salem jail three months later, Marshal Herrick
thrusts Sarah Good and Tituba out of a cell so that Danforth
and Hawthorne may confer there. The two women, leaving, chatter crazily of good times with the Devil in sunny Barbados. The
jail stench is foul, Herrick is drunk, and confusion and misery
are rife in Salem. Hale has been ministering to those about to
hang, and Parris looks gaunt and a little mad. Abigail and her
friend Mercy fled Salem recently, taking money from his strong-
box with them. Broken, Parris pleads for a postponement of the
executions, especially of the much respected Proctor and Rebecca,
but the judges remain obdurate. Hale says that none will confess,
despite his efforts.

In hopes that she will induce Proctor to admit his guilt, Elizabeth is brought in. She is thin, pale, and dirty, but retains a quiet dignity. Hale, horrified at the havoc everywhere, urges her to get John to lie. John then arrives, bearded, grimy, and worn, having been kept chained in the dungeon. They talk privately, and he is saddened to learn that Giles Corey is dead. The old man was pressed with great stones, since he would not plead in a way that would surely disinherit his sons.

Proctor declares that he is not a saint like Rebecca, and asks Elizabeth how she would feel if he lied to save his life. Humbly, she refuses to judge him, admitting that she, too, has sinned. Unsure of herself, she was cold to him, thus driving him into Abigail's arms.

Proctor decides to confess, and Hawthorne and the other judges are delighted. He does not like, however, their publishing his shame in the village and he adamantly refuses to name anyone else accusingly. He balks further at signing his name to the dishonorable confession. Then, with newfound courage, he joins the brave Rebecca and goes to his doom. Hale begs Elizabeth to call him back, but she will not take from him his painfully acquired "goodness." There is an ominous roll of drums, and Hale weeps.

ANALYSES OF THE MAJOR CHARACTERS

JOHN PROCTOR: This plain-spoken, vigorous farmer would seem to represent the good, average citizen who may upon occasion be moved to take heroic action. He would not normally be considered a saintly individual, and he has no great eagerness to be a martyr. Yet when put to the final test, the meaning here of "crucible," he will go to his death rather than irrevocably compromise his integrity.

His human frailty is established early in the play. Although normally a good husband and father, he is said to have seduced the beautiful and very young Abigail, when she was a servant girl at his farm. In a community that places much emphasis upon church attendance, he has not been the most faithful of worshippers. In addition, as the Reverend Mr. Hale easily ascertains, he cannot readily recite his Ten Commandments.

Furthermore, he is by no means desirous of courting trouble. He may speak up boldly to Parris, for whom he has contempt, but he is decidedly cautious when questioned by Hale. Whatever private opinions he entertains on the subject of witchcraft, he makes his replies as ambiguous as possible to avoid drawing the minister's censure. He also tries to stop Elizabeth from speaking too freely.

On three other occasions there is abundant evidence that he is not naturally given to rash or bold gestures. For one thing, he is quite reluctant to heed his wife's urging to denounce Abigail to the court. Apart from the fact that he has loved her, he considers the move dangerous. He might not be believed. Again, when the judges tell him that he need not keep forcing upon them the un-welcome deposition, since his wife claims to be pregnant, he is, for the moment, unsure. Clearly he is tempted to withdraw, but loyalty to his friends finally wins out. Lastly, after suffering torture and close confinement for several months, he is disposed to sign a confession. This is not entirely selfish, for he wants to care for his wife and children. Yet it is consistent with his over-all inclina-tion to avoid heroics. He himself says that since he is not of heroic mold, it would almost be hypocritical of him to stand up and play the hero.

In spite, however, of his humble awareness of guilt and unwilling-ness to run foolishly into jeopardy, he is a forceful individual given to decisive action. He bluntly opposes Parris and Putnam. He tears up Herrick's warrant and tries to prevent the officers from arresting and chaining his wife. He works extremely hard to get Mary Warren to change her story, and joins with Nurse and Corey in obtaining the deposition favoring the accused wo-men. When all else fails, he speaks up and reveals his shameful act of adultery to the judges. Even in prison he does not accept defeat easily. He struggles bravely until restrained by fetters, and will talk to no one, only deigning occasionally to take some food.

When, therefore, he suggests toward the end that only in destroy-ing his lying confession does he reveal some goodness, he is not being fair to himself. He has hitherto fought hard and ably for justice; and in admitting publicly his sin with Abigail to save Eliza-beth, he has already shown himself capable of generous self-sacrifice. Because he has a lively conscience, he may, in fact, have followed Elizabeth's lead and undervalued his own merits because of his one sensual lapse.

At the same time, when he must choose either the lie and life, or the truth and death, he is understandably uncertain. Certain factors, however, combine to help him arrive at his final noble decision. First of all, Elizabeth, while giving him no directive, lets him know that she thinks him a good man. And she herself, of course, has not surrendered. Secondly, he is more than ever impressed with the fanatical harshness of the judges. They will leave him no shred of self-respect if he yields. Thirdly, he thinks of his children and dreads willing them a dishonored name. Fourthly, he is shamed by the courage of Rebecca and the others who have not freed themselves by lying. Fifthly, he feels, as before, a strong sense of loyalty. He certainly will not implicate his friends in any confession. But will not any confession be a form of disloyalty? Finally, he comes to see that his own consciousness of integrity is supremely important. And it is this sudden awareness —that he cannot even to save his life deny all that he stands for —that enables him to leave his now-more-than-ever beloved wife and accept his fate with courage.

Proctor, of course, is not altogether "average." He is, from the first, a forceful individual. But only after much suffering and painful doubt does he recognize fully his dignity as a man and defend his truth to the death.

ELIZABETH PROCTOR: Elizabeth is sometimes in the play called Goody Proctor, the word "Goody" being a conventional title for a married woman. She is first mentioned by the hostile Abigail as being a cold, bitter liar. Afterwards the beautiful and passionate Abby attacks her again to John Proctor himself. And while he loyally defends his wife, he does not seem entirely to disagree.

In Act II, Elizabeth herself appears and does little at first to make a much more favorable impression. She goes about her household duties with an injured air and finally provokes even the penitent Proctor's anger with her stony, unforgiving manner. She is perhaps trying to be more agreeable, and she has undoubtedly been hurt by his infidelity. But when she urges him to go and denounce Abigail, she is almost too ready to see in his understandable hesitation more evidence of his weakness.

In the scene with Hale, however, Elizabeth begins to win more sympathy. She shows more spirit than Proctor in rejecting any suggestion that she has failed in her religious obligations. She has lived up to her creed and knows it. If she can be thought a witch, then there is no such thing as witchcraft. Afterwards when the men come to arrest her, she speaks up firmly about Mary's poppet or doll. Faced with the inevitable, however, she leaves with quiet dignity, having first left instructions about the care of the house and the children. Actually, she is afraid, but resolutely declares that she will not fear.

She measures up well, also, when she is summoned to court. It is known already that she has made no confession but has informed the court promptly of her pregnancy, probably aware that they might not readily execute a woman expecting a child. Respected by her husband because she has always told the truth, she is suddenly called upon, without warning, to testify as to his relationship with Abigail. Whatever she may have said to him in private, Elizabeth cannot bring herself to injure John's reputation.

She stretches the truth as far as possible and thus, ironically, destroys his chance to defeat Abigail. Here, however, it is clear that Elizabeth loves her husband enough to go against her own strict code.

In her final appearance it becomes evident that as a result of her cruel imprisonment she has become wiser, more understanding. She has come to appreciate John's goodness, whereas formerly she saw only his betrayal. In addition, she has recognized her own part in his fall from grace. Because she was unsure of herself, believing she was plain and unattractive, she was tense and anxious, as well as easily jealous. Had she been warmer, more loving, he might not have strayed.

Elizabeth has also realized, however, that she cannot tell her husband what to do. For one thing, she no longer feels so ominiscient and above reproach. For another, she knows that he must settle matters with his own conscience. Loving him now more than ever, she desperately wants him to live and knows that she can probably persuade him to do so. Yet having assured him that she will respect him whatever he decides, she heartbrokenly refuses to urge him to follow Hale's counsel of compromise. This means exercising iron control, but Elizabeth knows that John must achieve some peace of soul even if it means his death. Always a good woman, she too achieves here an act of heroic renunciation.

JOHN HALE: The Reverend Mr. Hale, minister of Beverly, is another character who moves from a comforting sense of goodness and capability to a humbling awareness of limitations. When he arrives at the Parris home with his arm-load of learned volumes, he is in the best of spirits. He knows that whatever problems may have arisen to disturb these worthy but uninformed villagers, he has all the answers. He may have to investigate carefully and sift evidence. He realizes that some may not have his training and not be so apt at separating truth from falsehood. But he will be patient, tolerant, and firm until all mists are cleared away. Hale, in short, is seen at first as a well-meaning but conceited young man of learning.

His vulnerability soon becomes apparent. He talks much of sifting facts and consulting reliable sources. But he also has high hopes of getting prompt, impressive results. Hence when the startling, highly emotional revelations of Tituba shock the assemblage, he jumps at the chance for a showy conversion and orders those accused into irons. Proctor and Rebecca have already urged caution; there are obvious tensions between them and the Putnams; Abigail has already been proved to have engaged in questionable activities; and Tituba is a terrified slave. Yet Hale exaltedly announces that the powers of evil have been defeated.

By Act II, however, he is less certain. Events he helped to set in motion are now causing him anxiety. So he comes by night to question the Proctors. He is somewhat severe with John because of his poor record of church attendance, but he is impressed with his sensible manner and shaken when he accuses Abigail of fakery. He is also favorably disposed toward Elizabeth after hearing her spirited defense of her life as a conscientious Christian woman. So he is surprised and disturbed when the marshal comes to arrest her. Proctor, of course, suspects that he came to trap them. But Hale avows his ignorance and promises to speak on her behalf. He still, however, declares that the courts are just and will free the innocent. Actually, he feels guilty and uncertain. He cannot see how one girl like Abigail could cause so much havoc, and he does not want to accept Proctor's angry charge that he, Hale, is a coward. Much troubled, he takes refuge in the theory that the whole village must in some way have offended God and thus drawn down divine wrath.

From then on he tries to be of some help to Proctor and his friends. He makes excuses for Proctor's Sunday plowing, and mentions the over-all panic to explain why some fear to give evidence. He suggests that the men's petition be placed in a more acceptable legal form, and urges that Mary Warren's accusations against Abigail be very carefull weighed. When Elizabeth's reticence weakens John's case against Abigail, Hale again comes to John's defense, claiming that he has always suspected Abigail of lying. Unimpressed with the final screaming that causes Proctor's arrest, he walks out of the court, denouncing the proceedings.

It might then be assumed that Hale turns into an admirable figure. After one act of folly, he perceives his error and tries to save those accused. Yet in the long run Hale, for all his decent instincts, comes off badly because he represents the side of unworthy compromise. Having failed to obtain any postponement of the executions, he pleads with those condemned to make lying confessions. His argument is that no faith justifies the sacrificing of life, God's most precious gift. Those who will not yield, even under such impossible conditions as those prevailing in Salem, may be damned for pride. Elizabeth replies that he thus takes the Devil's side. Despite his urging and her own love for Proctor, she will not accept his teachings. And at the end, she, recognizing John's heroism, stands inspired, while Hale weeps.

As compared then with the stern, heartless Danforth and Hawthorne, Hale is more human, more open-minded, and more capable of admitting that he could be wrong. He also shows some courage in coming to the defense of the Proctors and in irately quitting the court. Yet, when measured against the uncompromising valor of Corey, Rebecca Nurse, and both Proctors, he is seen as a moral failure. A minister pledged to uphold the truth, he counsels deliberate lying, and his emotional reasoning rings false. Harshly tested, as are the rest, he denies his principles, and is last seen a pitiable lost man, rejected by all.

MARY WARREN: This weak, frightened young girl plays a more crucial role in the play itself than the domineering Abby. She is not mean or vindictive. Neither is she callous, for she comes home sick and horrified when the first executions are set. She also does make some attempt to stand up bravely and confess her "pretense."

Usually, however, she tends to yield to stronger personalities. Badly frightened when Abby threatens, she jumps when ordered home by the angry Proctor. For a brief time, of course, she does make a pathetic effort to assert her dignity as someone of importance. She is a court official who had dined with the great and cannot be sent to bed like an unruly child. But her confidence quickly evaporates, and she is bewildered and alarmed when the poppet Abby induced her to give her mistress is produced as evidence of witchcraft.

Like John Proctor himself, she mistakenly assumes that all her false testimony in court was a simple matter of lying. Yet she cannot seem to simulate one more fainting spell when so commanded by the judge. Actually, as in the subsequent episode in which she screamingly denounces Proctor, she is probably at times hysterical. When under Abby's baleful influence, being timorous anyway by nature, she undoubtedly is often a prey to uncontrollable emotions.

ABIGAIL WILLIAMS: Abigail is shown generally as a cool, resourceful schemer taking advantage of a peculiar situation to advance her own plans. At the outset it is not at all clear why she led the midnight revels in the forest. Idle and restless since her dismissal from the Proctors, she undoubtedly craves excitement. She may, however, also have had some belief in Tituba's magic. Betty Parris says that Abby drank blood as a charm to kill Elizabeth.

When questioned, she weighs answers carefully, telling as little as necessary, hotly defending her virtue in general, and blaming everyone else whenever she can. The plot involving Mary's presentation of the doll is well planned and executed, and she seems to have no compunction about causing others to die. She has been, in her opinion, badly treated, and she will brazenly cut down any who now challenge her veracity. She even warns the formidable judge, Danforth, that in questioning her he may be calling down upon himself God's wrath for allowing Hell to confuse him.

In the early scene with Proctor, it is true, she does give some hint of softer feelings. He has, she says, taught her how to love, and she lives only for the embraces he has since denied her. Shortly afterwards, however, she is cleverly fending off Hale's questions. Abigail once tells the girls by way of threat that she knows how to provide a "pointy reckoning," having seen her own parents brutally slain by Indians. And she subsequently proves herself a dangerous foe, until the day she flees Salem with her friend Mercy and her uncle's carefully hoarded savings.

One final question remains. Is Abigail herself, for all her cold plotting, sometimes partly hysterical? Her outcries following Tituba's confession have in them a note of wild glee. And when, under great tension later, she turns on Mary Warren, she seems genuinely frightened and her hands are icy. Abby is, in general, the hard opportunist who leads the young accusers. But the Putnams and other older villagers are also stirring up enmities. And it is possible that she, too, is sometimes caught up in the feverish excitement that grips all of Salem.

REBECCA NURSE: This aged and revered grandmother is used throughout to point up the criminal absurdity of Salem's witchcraft proceedings. Even before coming to Salem from Beverly, Hale has heard of her many charitable works. And when later he learns of her arrest, he is shocked. For if she should be proved corrupt, then nothing will prevent "the whole green world from burning."

As regards the outbreak of trouble, Rebecca is the peacemaker, trying to restore sanity and friendlier feelings. She soothes the screaming Betty by her very serenity and strength, without saying a word. And she urges the distraught Mrs. Putnam to worry less. Rebecca knows about excitable children and has seen most of their crises overcome with time and patience. When the Putnams continue to talk of witchcraft, she urges them to seek solace in prayer. This advice rouses their ire, since they envy her flourishing family.

She is quietly in agreement with Proctor's charge that Parris's fiery sermons discourage those with children from coming to church. But she tries to get the resentful Proctor to make his peace with Parris, regardless. She is horrified to learn that Goody Putnam sent a small daughter to conjure with Tituba, and she hopes that Hale's strenuous efforts to drive out demons will not hurt the little Parris girl. When she leaves them to go to her prayers, they all know that she is not at all certain that good will be accomplished by Hale's ministrations.

In the last act, when Proctor must decide what course to take, he always has Rebecca as the standard of heroic silence. Others may break down, but the frail, aged Rebecca is a saint, already with "one foot in heaven." When she is told that John has confessed, Rebecca is stunned. She could not tell a lie to damn herself. How could he? And the moral force she exerts helps to make him change his mind. Rebecca is last seen, feebly but with courage, going to her death, with Proctor holding her arm. He now repays with physical support the moral support she has given him.

COMMENTARY ON *THE CRUCIBLE*

LUKEWARM RECEPTION: First produced in New York in January, 1953, *The Crucible* received less acclaim than Miller's two earlier works. The favored young playwright of that season was William Inge, whose *Picnic* took both Critics' Circle and Pulitzer awards. To be sure, the play was widely discussed. The term "witch hunt," during the previous decade, had been used frequently in American political discussions. And many seemed prepared to find Miller's play about early Salem a simple allegory about current conditions. This preoccupation with the work's possible political message gave it the current-interest appeal of any controversial piece. Yet it also tended to curtail consideration of the work strictly as a serious drama. Significantly, during the last ten years, as some of the more heated political controversies of that time have ceased to be dominant, the play itself has been increasingly admired. It has been often revived successfully. Many schools and colleges have presented it, an off-Broadway production was quite successful, and a leading repertory company trouped it across the country.

One source of disappointment to many Miller admirers was the play's relatively conventional form. After seeing *Death of a Salesman*, they looked forward to new experiments in form, new and freer styles of expression. *The Crucible*, however, with no startling violation of chronological order, moved from village bedroom to farm, then to court and prison. In point of fact, there were some interesting departures. The four-act structure itself was unusual. And the first act, called "An Overture", gave general background, but did not clearly single out the Proctors, around whom most of the later action would revolve. For a skilled playwright this was a rather daring move, but Miller was attempting to get his audiences well steeped in the very different atmosphere of a bygone era before setting up his central conflict. Not all have reacted favorably to this method. Some have felt that it makes for a weaker plot structure and a less unified, more diffuse work. But this was at least another experiment of sorts in adapting a dramatic form.

The language, too, is not that of *All My Sons* and *Death of a Salesman*. For the dialogue, Miller often worked in older patterns of speech. For example: "I never kept no poppets, not since I were a girl," or "Be you foolish, Mary Warren? Be you deaf?" or again, "No, it rebels my stomach," or "We cannot blink it more." The playwright's problem here was to create lines that would suggest the atmosphere of a much earlier America and yet be clear and meaningful to contemporary audiences. At the same time, the unfamiliar idioms or verb forms could not be so intrusive that they would distract attention constantly from the dramatic business at hand. This is by no means an easy feat to accomplish. Miller did, however, develop a forceful medium that sounds strong, simple, and direct and yet has the picturesque quality of a slightly strange or foreign way of speaking. And this, too, proved that Miller was not giving up his earlier concern with working out new methods of theatrical expression.

POWERFUL CONFLICTS. Miller is a playwright who deals seriously with what he considers the crucial issues of our time. As has already been indicated, *The Crucible* struck many viewers from the first as a "message play" about the then current political situation in America. Apart, however, from its intellectual aspects concerned with social criticism, it has scenes that are remarkably absorbing. The whole matter of witchcraft and strange rites in the forest by night has a certain theatrical glamor about it. And the questioning of Tituba, climaxed by her highly emotional and imaginative confession, is always exciting.

The second act has the tense, charged scene in which the Proctors, uneasy and at odds, uncomfortably join forces to avoid the dangers in Hale's questions. The incident of Mary Warren's rag doll is also handled for maximum suspense; and the act ends with John's violent reaction to the startling order of arrest.

Act III has the lively interest of any good courtroom scene, with stern judges, agonized defenders, and death sentences pending. Here the struggle over Mary Warren's change of testimony is extremely effective, winding up with the screaming hysterics of the girls. And there is considerable suspense when Elizabeth is summoned to confirm or deny her husband's admission of infidelity.

In the final act there is the dread atmosphere of impending executions. And there is question enough up to the end as to how John Proctor will finally decide. As in plays about Joan of Arc, the episode of the confession submitted and then revoked is certain to sustain interest.

Throughout the conflicts are strong, and much good drama is a matter of struggles between characters. Rebecca and the Putnams, Parris and John, John and Elizabeth, John and Abigail, Hale and the other judges—again and again sharp words make for lively action.

POLITICAL BACKGROUND. During the years before the play was first presented, Congressional committees had been probing the question of un-American activities. There was much controversy in the country about the work of such committees and especially of the Senate investigative group headed by Senator Joseph McCarthy of Wisconsin. Those favoring the operation asserted that those hostile to our way of life had attempted systematically to obtain key positions in government and in such influential industries as communications and entertainment in order to subvert our system. They therefore insisted that for the general welfare it was essential that all with such traitorous leanings be identified and removed from areas where they could presumably do effective damage.

Those opposed to the investigations tended to dismiss the element of threat to national security as negligible. They expressed much more concern over possible infringements of the rights of those subject to questioning. They accused committee members of frightening the American people unnecessarily in order to further their own political ambitions. And they warned that such probing might give encouragement to lying informants anxious to further their own interests or to revenge personal injuries. On the whole, then, they found the methods and procedures of the committees objectionable, and referred angrily to "McCarthyism." They also doubted that dangerous traitors were any more prevalent than real witches were during the Salem trials, and so referred to the investigations as "witch hunts."

Miller deals with investigations in both *The Crucible* and *After the Fall,* and obliquely with Nazi interrogations in *An Incident at Vichy.* In *After the Fall,* he refers directly to Congressional hearings. In the interim between 1952, when *The Crucible* was copyrighted, and 1964, when *After the Fall* was produced, Miller himself had been called before a Congressional Committee. He appeared in 1956 and denied having been under Communist discipline. His statement was accepted, but he was later cited for contempt because he refused to name those seen at writers' meetings under leftist auspices. This conviction for contempt was later reversed by the Appeals Court.

Even in the early fifties, however, Miller was far from favorably disposed toward the activities of the investigators. *The Crucible* is not a simple allegory attacking their goals and methods. Miller seems to have been genuinely interested in the historical Salem situation itself, and to have done much painstaking research to recreate a remote and quite different civilization. Hale, Hawthorne, and Proctor are thus no mere false fronts for easily identifiable twentieth-century personalities.

Yet, to put it simply, Miller paints the Salem investigations as running an evil course and creating havoc. And the viciousness, stupidity, self-seeking, and mob hysteria he links with the trials then are largely similar to charges leveled against the twentieth-century probes by all who disapproved of the Congressional hearings. While never specifically or crudely drawn, the parallels are there and clearly so intended. And the heroes, like Proctor and Rebecca, who bravely assert their innocence before tribunals, are cruelly sent to their deaths.

INTERPRETATION OF HISTORY. Although he uses a dramatist's prerogative to handle material freely, Miller deals largely with known historical figures. There was, for instance, a real Rebecca Nurse (or Nourse), as this commentator knows from family history. She was the wife of Francis; they did have many children and grandchildren, and they had been involved in local disputes with hostile neighbors. Rebecca was among those hanged, and there was much feeling at the time that the execution of such an estimable older woman proved how absurd the judicial pronouncements had become. Proctor, Corey, Parris, and the Putnams were also historical, and Judge Hawthorne was an ancestor of the later well-known writer, Nathaniel Hawthorne.

Yet in handling this historical material, Miller had to decide what to make of the proceedings. For one thing, the trials dealt with possible supernatural manifestations, and some might choose to emphasize the religious implications. Miller, however, while admitting that certain unleashed destructive forces can wreak almost unbelievable havoc, tends to show us the troubles as stemming from certain recognizable human failings. He provides us, in other words, with a set of secular or natural explanations. They may be summed up as follows:

1. GREED. Parris has resented all attempts to limit his acquisitions, and Putnam is avidly seeking more and more land.

2. VENGEANCE. Abigail wants to destroy Elizabeth Proctor. Martha Corey is accused by a man to whom she once sold an ailing pig.

3. JEALOUSY. Mrs. Putnam, with only one child, begrudges Rebecca her large, flourishing family. Abigail is jealous of Elizabeth.

4. AMBITION. Hale is clearly anxious to be known as a learned man who can solve difficult problems with ease. Abigail and Mary Warren both enjoy being treated with deference.

5. FEAR. Abigail and the girls fear the consequences both of the original forest dance and the later possible disclosure that they have lied. Tituba fears for her life and confesses. Mary Warren fears both John and Abigail. The good people of Salem who sign the petition do so with hesitation and have to be assured that they will not be called to testify. Others confess to avoid execution.

6. HYSTERIA. Both in the scene in which Tituba confesss and in that in which Abigail and the girls frighten Mary Warren into rejoining them, there is the suggestion of uncontrolled emotions carrying along a whole group to behave unreasonably.

MAJOR THEMES

1. PERSONAL LIBERTY. In his introductory comments, Miller notes that all governments must restrain to some extent the freedom of individual subjects or citizens. Sometimes, as was true when the early colonists had to face incredible dangers, tighter controls may have been useful. But it is often hard for authorities to realize, Miller believes, when the no-longer-necessary restraints should be relaxed. In his play about Salem, those in charge are ruthless in suppressing all opposition. Note how all-but-impossible it is for Corey, Nurse, and Proctor to have their evidence received. They are promptly and unjustly accused of trying to undermine the court itself. Thus, one idea in *The Crucible* is that governments should not be so overzealous in potecting themselves as to roughly violate individual rights.

2. NEED FOR INTEGRITY. Such undesirable tendencies can only be counteracted when those affected refuse courageously to be silenced. Hale speaks in favor of compromise. Do what the oppressors want and bide for time. Do anything rather than suffer death. But Hale's counsel is rejected as the mere rationalizing of cowardly behavior. Corey, Elizabeth, John and Rebecca all eventually stand fast. And the implication is that even if they suffer for their bravery, they provide the only hope for the restoration of justice. In addition, it is further suggested that the decent individual cannot achieve any happiness by failing to act according to what he knows is right. Hale is obviously miserable, whereas the Proctors and Rebecca achieve an exalted sense of having lived up to their ideals.

3. THE HUMAN BOND. In *All My Sons*, Keller is judged severely for having placed the limited interests of his family above all that he also owed to fellow human beings in general. Much, too, will be made of this human tie in *An Incident at Vichy*. Here, Abigail clearly thinks only of her personal concerns, as apparently does Putnam. Twice Proctor is tempted. Once, when the judges assure him that Elizabeth's pregnancy will rule out any immediate execution, he thinks of withdrawing. Again, when he thinks of his wife and children, he is inclined to confess. In both instances, however, he remembers his friends and considers the over-all effect of his actions. He then makes a nobler choice.

REVIEW QUESTIONS AND ANSWERS

I. Compare the characters of John Proctor and John Hale as they are gradually developed in *The Crucible*.

ANSWER: At the outset, Proctor and Hale are both vigorous young men in their thirties. Hale is a trained scholar, and Proctor is a farmer who cannot easily recite the Commandments. Both, however, exude confidence. Proctor talks quite assertively to Parris and Putnam. Hale is quite sure that he and his books can solve Salem's problems.

By Act II, both have been somewhat shaken. Proctor, having heard Mary Warren's account of the madness abroad, and being very uneasy about what Abigail may try next, answers Hale's questions quite cautiously. Hale, on his part, has undertaken the investigation because he is no longer quite so certain as he was when he ordered all those accused by Tituba and Abigail to be arrested and chained. He is impressed by the answers of the Proctors, and not at all pleased when Elizabeth is seized. But he wins Proctor's contempt as he tries to tell himself and the rest that justice will surely be done.

From then on Proctor fights valiantly to free his wife. Hale, however, tries to play both sides. He signs death warrants of those condemned, and yet he timidly does try to help Proctor and Nurse. Eventually he does angrily leave the proceedings, but his brave defiance comes too late.

At the end, Hale comes out firmly for moral compromise—lying to save one's life. And the Proctors reject his counsel as unworthy.

Thus, Proctor goes to his death with shining integrity. Hale lives, a beaten, rejected symbol of principles betrayed.

2. Why does the weak Mary Warren, rather than the ruthless Abigail, receive more attention in the play?

ANSWER: There are several reasons why this nervous, unstable girl is given so much prominence. First of all, in dramatic terms, the uncertain character makes possible more suspense. The very coldness and cleverness of Abigail that make her formidable also make any surprising change on her part unlikely. But Mary, essentially well-meaning and decent, is torn between her loyalty to the Proctors and her fearful dependence upon Abigail. The audience can, therefore, not be wholly sure which side she will finally support. This makes her an interesting figure.

In addition, she is used to illustrate how the weak can sometimes be used by more dominating, unscrupulous individuals to bring about grave injustices. Mary Warren is sick with horror at the idea of the death warrants. Moreover, her gift of the doll to Elizabeth seems to have been well meant. But she has clearly been used as a pawn to get her mistress convicted of witchcraft. Later, when Abigail starts the outcry against her, she screams out her accusations against Proctor largely from hysterical terror. She then simply cannot help herself.

Finally, the character is used to bring out how valueless may be the testimony of the badly frightened. Mary Warren may wish to be a good girl and not lie. Yet she cannot pretend to faint. On the other hand, virtually against her will she may launch terrible accusations. Evidence must be evaluated whence it comes. And even the well-intentioned, the play suggests, may be caught up in the hysteria of the moment and do inestimable damage.

3. What is the significance of the title, *The Crucible?*

ANSWER: A crucible is literally a container used in the process of heating and melting metals. When subjected to great heat while in such a container, the more valuable metals are separated from the baser. When used figuratively, the word "crucible" means a hard test or severe trial.

In this play, not metals but men and women are made to undergo a sort of smelting process. When the Proctors, the Coreys, and Rebecca Nurse are arrested and forced to face dreadful accusations, they are in effect told to confess or die.

These people do not want to lose their lives. On the other

hand, they are not accustomed to swearing to what is untrue. Their religion tells them that in doing so they court damnation. And even their ordinary self-respect normally demands of them that they speak the truth and keep their word. Yet if they will "confess" and satisfy their judges, they can live. If they tell the truth, they will be hanged. For average farm people not used to thinking of themselves as heroes, this is a formidable choice to have to make.

Despite some natural hesitation, however, the Proctors, Rebecca, and Giles all live up to their code. Choosing death rather than perjury, they prove themselves to be the most precious metals in the American ore.

4. The first act of *The Crucible* is subtitled an "overture." Why is it so designated, and how has it been received critically?

ANSWER: The term "overture" means normally an opening or introductory part of a musical composition or a literary work. In a sense, of course, any play's initial scenes must be concerned with giving necessary background material and identifying characters and situations so that the audience can follow the plot. But in this drama the procedure is somewhat different.

Although *The Crucible* has several extremely admirable figures, the main character or actual hero would seem to be John Proctor. Along with most of the other leading participants in the central conflict, Proctor does appear in the first act or overture. But he by no means stands out as he does during the rest of the play. Moreover, much of the later action will deal with the complex relationship between him and his wife, Elizabeth. But Goody Proctor, while mentioned, does not appear in this opening act at all.

In setting up *The Crucible*, Miller was very much aware of the differences between the theocratic civilization of seventeenth-century New England and the more secularist society of our own times. So he decided to give a great deal of background and establish well his period atmosphere before setting the Proctor plot fully in motion. Some critics have felt that this postpones unnecessarily the main action of the play. Others have commended the dramatist for taking a novel approach in solving the technical problems in this unique work.

5. What dramatic purposes are served by the role of Giles Corey?

ANSWER: Cranky, obstreperous old Giles adds, first of all, an element of humor to a generally somber drama. A rather fussy, eccentric character, he is proud of his many bouts with the law, much to the amusement of his friend Proctor and the annoyance of the grimly acquisitive Putnams.

Secondly, Giles, with his innocent but foolish questions, is used to show on what absurd pretexts charges might be leveled against harmless people, once the fear of witchcraft had been roused. Much gratified to be able to get a bit of free information from the learned visitor, the Reverend Mr. Hale, Giles inquires why his wife Martha is always reading books that she will not let him see. Later, when Martha has been arrested, the heartbroken old man will rue his unfortunate remarks. Yet in more normal times, no one at all would have taken his querulous complaints seriously at all.

Finally, he emerges, for all his cantankerous quirks, as a man of integrity and courage. Having given his word to protect his source for the accusation against Putnam, he refuses to divulge the name even when accused of contempt. And he goes to his painful death in silence, refusing to plead at all, in order to protect the rights of his children. Tested in the crucible of the witchcraft trials, this crotchety old farmer acquits himself well as a decent human being.

6. When Proctor, Nurse, and Corey try to introduce evidence for the defense, why is their attempt doomed almost from the start?

ANSWER: Some of their difficulties seem to stem from the court procedures of the time, which apparently were not designed to protect adequately the rights of those accused. But there are other factors also operating against them.

First of all, there is the nature of the witchcraft charge. As is pointed out by the judges, since the alleged offense involves matters of subtle spiritual influences, ordinary rules of evidence cannot apply. A person, in theory, could apparently be peaceably at home minding his own affairs, and yet be sending his spirit out to harass someone else. Great reliance would therefore be placed upon the word of the presumed victim.

Secondly, the presence of fear in both community and court helps to hinder their efforts. The good people who could attest to the innocence of the women accused stay fearfully away from the proceedings and beg that no names of theirs be used, lest they in turn be arrested. And the judges themselves seem afraid. Perhaps the whole authority of the courts is being threatened by these angry petitioners. And again, should they be proved right, will this mean that the court has already condemned innocent people?

Thirdly, there are personal grudges involved. Parris certainly has no love for Proctor, who criticized him as unworthy to hold the town's religious services. Putnam is not only greedy for land, but is anxious to protect the reputation of his daughter, one of the girls making the charges. And Abigail wants her revenge against the Proctors and is also determined to avoid being charged herself.

Finally, there are two almost accidental elements that help wreck the Proctor case. Normally, Elizabeth would tell the whole truth, and Proctor would be safe in avowing that she would validate his confession. For once, however, her wifely compassion acts to make her at least stretch the truth a bit to save her husband's good name. And this half-lie ironically helps to doom him. Moreover, were Mary Warren a slightly stronger personality, she might not have recanted her testimony. But, being a frightened, neurotic girl, she is easily dominated by the inexorable Abigail.

7. How does the relationship of John and Elizabeth change throughout the play?

ANSWER: In the first scene with Abigail, John firmly announces that he will not in the future prove unfaithful to his wife; but he does not with any great conviction deny the girl's charge that his wife is cold and severe. In Act II, Proctor is seen humbly trying to conciliate Elizabeth, but she remains frosty and clearly resentful. As a result, Proctor finally becomes angry and protests the harsh manner in which she never lets him forget his act of infidelity.

Once Hale arrives, however, to question the couple, the atmosphere begins to change. Whatever their private differences, John and Elizabeth are united in their efforts to convince the minister of their solid Christian convictions. And when Elizabeth becomes rather dangerously candid in opposing some of the witchcraft proceedings, John tries to make her answer sound less provocative. When, subsequently, men come to arrest her, John tears up the warrant and tries in vain to stop them.

At the time of the trial, he proves that he has made every effort to get evidence to save her, and eventually even confesses his shame to secure her release. She, in turn, goes against her principles to avoid injuring his good name. By the last act, when both have suffered rigorous confinements, the love and admiration between them is more than ever obvious. Both know their faults and want only to take up life together again, with their now deepened insights. But John finally goes to his death for the truth, and Elizabeth heartbrokenly understands and commends his heroism.

8. Can *The Crucible* be legitimately classified as a social drama, as the term is customarily used?

ANSWER: Social dramas in the Ibsen tradition usually deal with current problems and make use of contemporary settings and characters. *The Crucible,* by contrast, is clearly an historical work, and there is no reason to assume that it is some simple allegory exactly mirroring any modern situation. Yet it still fulfills certain requisites of social drama.

First of all, the questions that it raises, while not exclusively applicable to any era, are, or at least have been, of vital interest in our day. While people today have not been arrested for witchcraft, they have been accused of pursuing courses detrimental to the community. And there has been much discussion as to the validity of such charges and the methods employed in conducting related investigations. Since such matters involve both cherished individual rights and possible grave danger to the nation, a play like *The Crucible* can seem quite timely.

Furthermore, in other works, such as *All My Sons,* Miller has indicated the need for a thoroughly responsible citizenry at all times in order to safeguard the future of free men. Here the brave decisions of the Proctors and the other heroic characters are made to seem just as relevant to our own day as will be that of the Austrian prince in the most recent Miller drama, *Incident at Vichy.*

9. To what extent has Arthur Miller followed the facts of history in writing *The Crucible?*

ANSWER: In preparing his drama, the playwright engaged in extensive research; there is much in the play that is taken directly from the early history of New England. First of all, most of the leading characters were based upon people living in Salem at the time of the trials. John Proctor, Giles Corey, and Rebecca Nurse, as well as Parris, the Putnams, and the judges at the proceedings, were all taken from history. And the fate of Proctor and his friends is that of the originals. In addition, there is much valid information included as to the beliefs, customs, and practices of the time.

Certain elements, however, have been introduced to make the work more effective dramatically. Abigail has been made somewhat older, and there is no historic basis for the romance between her and John. As a result, the tensions existing between him and his wife were also invented by Miller. In fact, according to the playwright, only the skimpiest indications exist as to the character of John Proctor. So the playwright has done much to develop and reveal the personality of his hero.

Finally, there are doubtless some contemporary emphases. Miller himself has questioned whether or not the Proctors may be more aware of their own psychological states than would have been possible in their early era. And the language, although it sounds authentic, is essentially an effective stage idiom with period flavor.

10. Suggest some reasons why *The Crucible* is an effective drama on the stage, even apart from possible contemporary implications.

ANSWER: First of all, there are several scenes of strong conflict; and lively differences often form the basis for good theatre. Proctor and Corey align themselves against Putnam and Parris. John and Elizabeth have matters of disagreement; and Proctor takes issue with Mary Warren. The trial scene, of course, involves a number of bitter disputes; and then there is Proctor's final debate with the judges.

Secondly, good suspense is maintained. Inasmuch as the penalty for conviction in the trials is death, the stakes throughout are high. And at several points there seems to be some chance that injustice will be prevented. Will Mary Warren's testimony be accepted? Will Proctor's confession be confirmed by Elizabeth? Will Hale be able to postpone the executions? And then finally, of course, there is the question of Proctor's own decision.

Thirdly, there are quite a few attractive and appealing characters. The Proctors, old Giles, and Rebecca Nurse all have admirable human traits; and even Hale and poor Mary Warren win occasional sympathy. Ordinarily a play becomes more interesting if the audience cares about the characters. And as *The Crucible* proceeds, spectators find themselves much concerned with the fate of the men and women of principle whose lives are so unjustly in jeopardy.

A MEMORY OF TWO MONDAYS

(1955)

CHARACTERS

BERT. An eager, good-natured boy of eighteen, working in an auto-parts shipping room to save enough money to go on to college.

RAYMOND. The neat, slightly stooped manager, aged forty, who is concerned primarily with the efficient operation of his shipping room.

AGNES. A kindly, sympathetic spinster, who laughs easily.

PATRICIA. A flirtatious young assistant, who chatters about her dates and has an eye for Larry and Larry's new car.

GUS. A raucous, husky Slavic packer, in his late sixties, who enjoys a strenuous drinking bout but suffers deep remorse over having neglected his invalid wife.

JIM. A bespectacled elderly worker, who accompanies Gus on his wild sprees but maintains a dignified air.

KENNETH. A recent Irish immigrant, who quotes snatches of poetry, objects to off-color talk, and fears that poverty may at last induce him to bury himself in the Civil Service.

LARRY. A personable, rather worried auto-parts expert, nearly forty, who wants to take Patricia driving in his dream car, an Auburn with beautiful valves.

FRANK. A sturdy, matter-of-fact young truck driver, who seems mainly interested in making calls upon women who welcome him to various parts of the city.

JERRY and WILLIAM. Two rather impudent young workers, nattily attired, who are given to smart, cynical witticisms that irritate the others.

TOM. A slim, graying family man, who alarms loyal co-workers by coming to work so intoxicated as to risk being discharged.

MECHANIC. A customer in search of a rarely available auto part that only the knowledgeable Larry is able to locate.

MR. EAGLE. The shrewd, well-dressed boss, in his forties, who gives Tom a second chance with astonishing results.

SETTING

This short piece takes place in a rather grimy New York auto-parts warehouse shipping room during the Depression years. The set is supposed to appear both musty and disorderly, and at the same time somewhat strange and romantic. Although two different Mondays, perhaps a year apart, are described, there is no complete break in the action. The time lapse is suggested by a few poetic lines and by changes in the lighting.

PLOT ANALYSIS

Bert and the manager, Raymond, are the earliest arrivals at the shipping room on the first Monday. Bert, eighteen and ambitious, reads *War and Peace* on the subway and dreams of going to college. Most of his co-workers, however, seem rooted for life in their present routine jobs. As the others come in, certain relationships are established. Young Patricia, a coquette who will flirt with anyone except leering old Gus, has apparently shown some interest in Bert. She also, however, listens with obvious interest when the married, good-looking Larry talks of buying a new, smooth-running Auburn.

The two older cronies, Gus and Jim, come in after a weekend of heavy drinking. Though somewhat groggy, they are able to get around and handle their work. Not so Tommy Kelly. This gentle, graying clerk is so intoxicated that he appears half-asleep, stupefied. His faithful friends, having heard of the imminent visit of their boss, Mr. Eagle, vainly try to rouse him. In desperation, they finally prop him up and pretend to be talking over orders with him. Eagle, however, summons him ominously. And there is much fear that this well-liked family man may be dismissed. But to everyone's relief, Eagle gives him one more chance.

Although the other workers are all friendly enough, Bert is drawn to Kenneth, the only other kindred soul who might know a bit of verse. Kenneth is often taunted by the men with rougher, cruder senses of humor because he calls for decency and decorum, especially with women present. Lamenting that the shipping room is so dark and dingy, he and Bert finally make the daring decision to wash the windows.

But before they do so, there is bad news for Gus. While he and Jim were off on their weekend alcoholic fling, Gus's wife, Lilly, long an invalid, met her death. Gus is stunned and repents bitterly that he was not home with her at the time. He leaves, and work resumes. Then Kenneth and Bert wash the windows.

As they proceed with their task, time passes. Bert muses how sad it is that the same people keep doing the same job year after year. They have no ambition, and there seems to be little meaning in their dreary, uneventful lives. Bert cannot understand why Kenneth does not improve his prospects; but Kenneth confesses that he has not the persistence needed to reach a goal. Bert, however, he is certain, will go on to better himself.

During the period that has elapsed since the first Monday, some changes have occurred. Tommy, having learned his lesson, has given up drinking and become rather smug and sententious. Kenneth, on the other hand, is indulging too freely and has begun to forget his poetry. Larry, having sadly realized that Patricia does not really care for him deeply, is ready to sell his prized Auburn. And as for Gus, he still grieves brokenly for his wife. With a recklessness arising from despair, he goes on one last drunken fling, lavishly disposing of insurance money. Afterwards his saddened friends learn that he has been found dead in a cab.

The window-washing project was only moderately successful. It did mean more sunlight, but it also exposed to view the seamy activities in a nearby house of prostitution. The jests are vulgar, and Kenneth is outraged. But Eagle merely reminds him that he had to break precedent and wash windows. The time has come, however, for Bert to leave for college. All vaguely wish him well, but he realizes sadly that he has left little impression; and soon they will forget him entirely, even though this for him was a new, memorable experience.

ANALYSES OF THE MAJOR CHARACTERS

BERT: Eager and amiable, young Bert arouses mild interest on the part of his fellow workers because of his energy and ambition. Coming to work on the subway, he reads the *New York Times,* a newspaper with more comprehensive coverage and more detailed comment than the tabloids they would follow. In addition, he is working his way slowly through the long Russian novel *War and Peace,* by Leo Tolstoy. Although vaguely certain that Bert is thus certain to get ahead, they do not really understand his literary leanings, and as yet he is not very good at explaining what he hopes to achieve. He is tentatively reaching out for something better, whatever it may be, and is somewhat surprised that the others have so little urge to improve their respective lots.

In general, he gets along well with the others. He does good service, for instance, when all are trying to save the dazed Tommy Kelly from the disapproving notice of Mr. Eagle. Yet his closest companion there is obviously the Irish-born Kenneth, for the latter has also some interest in literature, as evidenced by his reciting snatches of poetry. Moreover, Kenneth also seems for a time to be rather ambitious. And Bert is glad to join him in washing the windows. Essentially, however, because he is young and determined to rise in the world, he has little in common with these fairly good-hearted, uneducated people who have settled down in routine work and have no strong urge to make a change. And Bert is saddened to think that his brief stay among them, to him a sort of exciting adventure, will scarcely even be remembered by this self-contained group.

KENNETH: As indicated above, Kenneth has the most immediate appeal to Bert because he likes poetry and reveals some longing for a better life. Even though desperately poor, he does not want to take too safe a civil service job because this would be a trap that might destroy all freedom and individuality. Yet while Kenneth, like Bert, has a vision of a more rewarding existence, he does not have Bert's strong determination. Hence, he cannot carry through any program of self-improvement, even though he talks of doing something and seems to want something more intellectually satisfying. Caught thus between his aspirations and his faltering will, he becomes increasingly frustrated and takes to drink. He talks more, does less, and even begins to forget the poetry that once gave a lift to his spirit. If Bert influences anyone during his short period of working with auto-parts, it is Kenneth, and not necessarily with happy results. For seeing the progressive young Bert, Kenneth finds his own ambitions stirred. But as Bert forges ahead, while he does not, his despair deepens and leads him to seek solace in alcohol.

GUS: This powerful, coarse, hard-drinking old workman is the last one to be ordinarily considered highly sensitive. He goes off on wild drinking sprees with an amiable crony, and jests roughly with the coquettish young Patricia. Yet the death of his invalid wife, while he was off carousing, fills him with deep remorse. He seems to himself to have failed in some solemn obligation, and he can no longer respect himself. So he scatters the insurance "blood money" among strangers in bars, makes meaningless but expensive phone calls, and dies pathetically in a taxi. Gus is somewhat like the tragic figures in other Miller plays, who must observe the demands of their personal code or die. Compromise is not for them.

COMMENTARY ON *A MEMORY OF TWO MONDAYS*

POOR RECEPTION. This short play by Arthur Miller opened in September, 1955, together with the somewhat longer *A View from the Bridge*. In general, the work was either lightly dismissed or altogether ignored. Miller himself has suggested than an inadequate opening-night performance on the part of a key member of the cast helped to create an unfavorable impression upon the critics. The playwright, however, has a special predilection for the piece, because it recreates certain vividly recalled experiences of his youth during the Depression era. For then he, too, like young Bert in the play, worked in an auto-parts warehouse to earn enough money to go on to college.

TECHNICAL VARIATIONS. Like most Miller dramas, this one includes interesting technical innovations. Earlier, in *Death of a Salesman,* the playwright had used flute music and subtle lighting to add an element of beauty and strangeness to a rather ordinary frame house in Brooklyn. As a result, Willy Loman's little home, dwarfed by surrounding tall apartments, was made to appear an almost dream-like family haven, recalling a more individualistic, semi-rural way of life now vanishing. In *A Memory of Two Mondays,* the scene is the shipping room of an auto-parts warehouse. It is a dusty, grimy place, with unwashed windows and minimal employee facilities. Yet again, through clever set designing, and subdued rather than harsh lighting, the effect is curiously attractive.

There are two apparent reasons for this approach. For one thing, the play is labeled "A Memory." Often, when an older person looks back at events that occurred when he was an eager, hopeful youth, he tends to remember the more pleasant aspects and endow all that happened with an aura of splendor and enchantment that may largely have been lacking at the time of the actual experience. Both *All My Sons* and *Death of a Salesman* have this nostalgic attitude toward the past. In *All My Sons,* Kate Keller almost dissuades the irate George from accusing her husband further, by recalling happier days in the old neighborhod. And the Salesman, Willy Loman, looks back to the days of glory years ago when his son Biff was a great high-school football star. In the other plays, characters are shown nostalgically referring to the past. Here, however, there is no present-day commentator. Yet the same softening perspective is achieved by technical devices.

Secondly, the special effects are intended to suggest what working together within the confines of this dreary loft can mean to a relatively congenial group. Their jobs may be routine and their prospects few. Yet life there is not altogether dull for any, even for those who lack Bert's aspirations. There is great excitement, for instance, as they get together to try to save poor, foolish Tommy Kelly's job. And then there is interest in Patricia's flirtations, Larry's new Auburn with the "nice valves," and Larry's astonishing feat of recalling where a hard-to-find part for an old truck is stored among cartons stacked on the third floor. Then, of course, there is concern over the death of Gus's wife. With steady work difficult enough to obtain during the Depression, the warehouse jobs mean necessary income for the other workers, as well as for Bert. But Miller's carefully planned set and lighting are meant to convey the idea that the old warehouse is a sort of world apart, in which this little group has its small but, to it, crucial experiences.

USE OF POETRY. Hitherto Arthur Miller had not employed poetry as such in dramatic works. Yet there was an obvious lyrical element in *Death of a Salesman*, and some of the dialogue in *The Crucible*, with its sinewy seventeenth-century eloquence, has the aura of poetry about it. But in *A Memory of Two Mondays*, verse is unmistakably introduced for special effects. Kenneth's snatches of older poems suggest his limited, but genuine, taste for something beyond the realm of cartons, labels, and rubber cement.

In addition, however, there are lines of free verse spoken by both Bert and Kenneth. Bert uses it when he sadly meditates upon the monotonous lives of workers like Gus, Agnes, and Tommy; and Kenneth, in turn, expresses poetically his own feelings of protest against the rigors of life in an American city for a poor man who has at least known what it is to "read a book through." Finally, Bert again speaks in verse when he thinks about his own forthcoming escape from routine drudgery, and pays almost rueful tribute to those who bravely go on with it year after year. At the same time, he is somewhat distressed to realize how little impression he will have made upon these people, whom he, curiously enough, will never forget. In all three instances, the tone is lyrical and elegiac or plaintive. And again, the dramatic contrast is striking between the solid, utilitarian character of the auto-parts business and the wistful aspirations of two who seek something to satisfy man's spiritual hunger.

SOCIAL DRAMA. In many ways, *A Memory of Two Mondays* is a nostalgic mood piece, rather than a work intended to criticize values in modern society. Yet there are here, as in most Miller plays, some incidental comments upon contemporary life. First of all, there is the suggestion of a regrettably low level of over-all cultural experience. These people are literate enough to scan tabloids, but get nothing from poetry or books in general. Their pleasures are seldom more exalted than the drinking spree or the casual affair.

In addition, there is no attempt to make their working conditions pleasant. The warehouse is grimy, its windows never cleaned. Rats consume some of the mailing supplies. And there is only one washroom for all who are on the premises. The boss is not cruel or inhuman. He even gives Tommy Kelly the one more chance he needs. But there is little in the warehouse picture to raise anyone's sights. Bert is young enough and determined enough to push on to something better. But Kenneth gradually loses his urge to improve his lot. He starts drinking heavily, as did Gus, Jim, and, formerly, Tommy. And he begins forgetting even the poems he once knew. As for Tommy, he does reform, but only to become less of a person, more of a smooth-functioning machine.

MODERN TRAGEDY. Again, the tragic element here is subdued, since this is not essentially a tragic drama. Yet when rough, burly Gus is so remorseful for having been out carousing when his invalid wife died, that he cannot forgive himself, he displays the intense, uncompromising spirit of some more fully developed Miller heroes. And Gus, of course, is again an ordinary man, distinguished only by the passionate way he clings to his own personal code.

There are, however, other tragic implications here. Bert and Kenneth have each had glimpses enough of a more beautiful world, beyond the confines of a warehouse, to want to extend the vision of their fellow workers. So, despite some rather discouraging jeers, they wash the windows to let in more light and air. Yet all that their co-workers actually seem to notice is the nearby house of prostitution. Had the results been more satisfactory, other improvements might have followed. But when this one effort fails, the implication is that the group, in general, will never be roused out of its apathetic state. It will go on, as Bert says, "riding back and forth across a great big room" without ever realizing how high the human spirit can soar. And their plodding along thus, "with no end in sight," seems to Bert, and probably to Miller, a tragic sort of existence.

REVIEW QUESTIONS AND ANSWERS

1. How is the crucial episode of the washing of the windows used to symbolize certain aspects of life among the warehouse workers?

ANSWER: First of all, it points up the difference between Bert and Kenneth and the rest. The others might vaguely agree that having more light and air would be desirable, but for years they have done nothing about it. They are accustomed to accepting resignedly the depressing surroundings in which they spend so many hours each week. Kenneth, of course, is somewhat different. He can still dream of the beauty of the "green countryside," and he has something of the poet's feeling for "God's light." But he would probably never make the move, were it not for Bert's energetic, encouraging presence.

But if Kenneth sees roses and a white cloud, and Bert admires a tree with red leaves and later the wonders of snow, the rest, untrained to focus attention on the changing natural scene, apparently ignore the operation altogether. Only when the prostitutes are sighted is any interest roused. Then Kenneth is appalled and would chivalrously protect Agnes and Patricia from the unpleasant scenes thus revealed. But the only response he gets from Mr. Eagle, the boss, is that probably the windows should never have been washed.

In a sense Bert and Kenneth are idealists, wanting to improve their own lot and that of others. But they get almost no support for their project from their lethargic group, and little thanks for their efforts. And even they must face the sad fact that the results are not quite what they anticipated. Yet for awhile at least the two of them did glimpse "a real summer sky."

2. Is Bert probably right in assuming that he will remember the other workers but that they will promptly forget him?

ANSWER: To Bert, the warehouse is a new and fascinating experience. This is his first contact with people whose entire lives are spent doing routine work, and he observes all that goes on with youthful interest and curiosity. Although he gets along well with the group and even garners praise for his help in shielding the drunken Tommy, he never really sees the job as more than a means of his getting away to college. And this sense of being there but briefly probably casts him even more in the role of the observer. Bert actually has a strong urge to extend his knowledge of the world. So everything is important to him, and he will not even take for granted ordinary occurrences that the rest have accepted for years. For instance, Bert is astonished at the extent of Larry's knowledge when Larry gives him explicit, if complicated, directions on where to find the rarely requested part for the old truck.

In addition, Bert is a reflective individual anyway. He may have trouble keeping awake over *War and Peace,* but he does think about the people he encounters. And he hates the dullness, the routine, the dust of the warehouse just enough himself to wonder a great deal about those who can tolerate it year after year with "no end in sight." He sees them always as a different species, and speculates about them with some amazement.

As for the others, they have long ceased to concern themselves much with the outside world at all. They live within their own dusty walls. While Bert is with them and almost one of them, they will pay him some small heed. But when he leaves, he goes on to become part of an unknown, more advanced group that is not their affair at all. Theirs are limited horizons.

3. Many of Miller's works have been discussed as psychological dramas. Can *A Memory of Two Mondays* be so classified?

ANSWER: Except for the death of Gus's wife, who, of course, is never met by the audience, and later of Gus himself, again offstage, there is little by way of an exciting story line here. The two Mondays are, to a great extent, average working days in an unspectacular business. The Monday morning hangovers, the office romance between Larry and Patricia, the fuss about washing the windows, all have a certain triteness about them that is not likely to generate much dramatic interest.

But all of this, in fact, is part of a "memory." It's presumably what Bert remembers and how he remembers it through the haze of years. And because Bert has a certain perspective, that of the eager, ambitious boy pausing momentarily to observe a way of life that seems to him very strange, even the routine events seem more suspenseful and more significant.

At the same time, even within the "memory," there is concern with the mental processes of characters. The washing of the windows, in particular, is meaningful only inasmuch as it reveals how Bert and Kenneth react to a situation, as opposed to how the rest of the group responds, or fails to respond. Bert wonders how these people can adjust to the terrible sameness of dreary tasks over long periods. He is also very much aware of the impression they are making upon him and of how very little he means to them. To sum up, this is psychological drama at least in the sense that the primary area of interest is the way different sorts of minds regard fairly commonplace happenings.

4. Select any five physical objects referred to in the play that have some symbolic value, and explain what they represent.

ANSWER: (1) Bert's copy of *War and Peace*. Regarded with mild curiosity and awe by Bert's fellow workers, this great Russian novel is used to suggest the boy's determination to improve his mind. It is a long work, and he is too tired to read much at a time. In fact, he is not yet very clear when he tries to explain what he hopes to glean from it. Yet he does make slow but sure progress, and he will presumably go on to complete his education.

(2) The Auburn. Larry's dream car, with the "nice valves," indicates that some spark of hope is still possible in this discouraged family man. Gradually, however, it becomes apparent that his interest in the car is somehow related to his romantic interest in Patricia. When the girl disappoints him, suddenly the idea of owning so expensive a machine seems "crazy," and now somehow "dead." So he will sell the Auburn, for he now knows that he can afford neither it nor the dream it signified.

(3) The part for the old truck. The problem suggests the Depression era when even antiquated machines would be used as long as possible. Apart from this, however, Larry's skill in locating the part awes young Bert. Yet Bert sees that although Larry has more knowledge about cars than he has, Larry will not "escape" to better surroundings, because he lacks Bert's determination to make progress.

(4) The pin. Patricia's new piece of jewelry indicates that she is flirting with Bert and others as well. Later she shows interest in Larry because of the car; but she is not ready to settle down with anyone. Patricia's unimpressive little affairs are such as to stir up some curiosity on the part of someone like Agnes, who has given up hope of ever getting married. But there is something dull and rather foolish about her and her successive romances. She is interesting only in that she is characteristic of a scene that Bert fondly remembers because it was once all so new to him.

(5) The windows. The grimy windows, that shut out all view of the world outside, suggest the closed-in lives of those who have little concern with anything beyond the small, dusty area in which they work. Bert and Kenneth wash the windows so that all may get sun and fresh air. These two want more than mere stagnating routine. Yet the clean windows only make it possible for their co-workers to note the prostitutes and make dubious jokes. Hence, the windows represent the view of life which an individual holds. If he wants to see more, he cleans the windows and may even catch a glimpse of what is beautiful. If he, however, is essentially incurious, he leaves the windows opaque, and even when someone else cleans them, looks out only when there is something crude or shocking. The sky, the tree, and the roses he never even sees.

A VIEW FROM THE BRIDGE

(1955, 1956)

CHARACTERS

ALFIERI. A stout, cheerful, middle-aged lawyer, born in Italy; thoughtfully amazed to discover, in his humble clients from the Brooklyn waterfront, mighty passions recalling their heroic ancestors.

EDDIE CARBONE. A good-natured, uneducated, hard-working longshoreman, fiercely determined to protect his young niece from those whom he regards, jealously, as unworthy suitors.

CATHERINE. His wife's attractive teen-aged niece, whom he has raised, and who is now eager, preferably with his blessing, to get herself a job or maybe marry the handsome young Rodolpho.

BEATRICE. Eddie's loyal but concerned wife, who realizes helplessly that her husband is dangerously overfond of her sister's little girl whom he so generously took in and educated.

MARCO. A strong, quiet-spoken cousin of Beatrice, entering America illegally to earn money for his wife and children in Italy— a man slow to anger, but formidable when once roused.

RODOLPHO. His blond, lighthearted young brother, whose singing and other artistic pursuits are, to the stubborn, possessive Eddie, unassailable proof that he would be no fit husband for Catherine.

LOUIS and MIKE. Two of Eddie's fellow longshoremen, rugged types; also somewhat suspicious of Rodolpho, but resentful enough of all authorities to shun bitterly any informer, Eddie included, who would bring about the young immigrant's arrest.

OTHER CHARACTERS. Among others who appear briefly are Mr. Lipari, the butcher, and his wife, who become incensed when Eddie's drastic act causes two of their relatives, also illegal arrivals, to be jailed, along with Marco and Rodolpho. In addition, there are the two immigration officers who make the arrest, as well as the two "submarines" they capture, and several neighbors who witness the final tragic confrontation.

SETTING

Divided into two acts, the play's events take place either in Alfieri's law office or in and around the Brooklyn tenement home of Eddie Carbone and his family. In the original Broadway production in

1955, the play was a fairly brief work and the apartment setting was fairly conventional. Afterwards, however, the playwright expanded the drama to full length. The longer version was produced in London in 1956 and appears in the *Collected Plays*. In 1965 this second treatment was presented off-Broadway in New York. At this time, a three-sided modified arena stage was used, with only the necessary chairs, tables, and a few props to suggest the Carbone apartment. In most instances, Alfieri, acting partially as chorus, sits at his desk to one side during the entire action.

PLOT ANALYSIS

ACT I. Alfieri, a stout, kindly lawyer in his fifties, remarks that the Brooklyn waterfront area has changed greatly since he first arrived from Italy twenty-five years ago. No longer do gangsters like Al Capone live violently in the slums near Brooklyn Bridge. Now the neighborhood is peaceable, and Alfieri normally handles only the routine petty cases of poor clients. Now and then, however, the old terrible passions are unleashed. There was, for instance, the matter of Eddie Carbone.

Eddie, a good-hearted, steady longshoreman, comes home from work and is warmly greeted by his young niece, Catherine. He likes her latest hair style and admires her new skirt, although it seems to him rather skimpy. She is grown up now, he warns her, and must walk with decorum to avoid the stares of men on the street. She is amused at his concern.

Soon afterwards he surprises his wife, Beatrice, with the word that her cousins, two "submarines" or illegal immigrants, have slipped into the country and will join them shortly. Bea wishes she had a new tablecloth. Eddie humorously agrees to give them shelter, on condition that he not be asked to give up his own bed. As they sit down to have dinner, Bea tells him that Catherine, hitherto in secretarial school, has been offered a job. Eddie does not want her to take it. She should finish her course. Besides, the position would bring her into another undesirable neighborhood. When, however, the girl looks crushed, Eddie reluctantly yields. He then warns them not to speak at all about the immigrants. Anyone suspected of playing informer pays the awful penalty of ostracism. They agree to be careful. He still wishes, however, that Catherine did not insist upon heading out to work. She is seventeen, still, to him, very young.

At ten the two cousins arrive. Marco, the elder, is a husky, quiet-spoken family man. Rodolpho, the younger, is blond, boyish, and carefree, and has learned to sing "Paper Doll." During the following weeks, Rodolpho and Catherine fall in love. Unconsciously jealous, Eddie urges Catherine to distrust the young Italian. He warns her that Rodolpho is using her only to obtain his citizenship papers more easily. After all, the young immigrant spends his money on a showy jacket, pointed shoes, and records. Is this responsible behavior? Catherine is unconvinced and avows that Rodolpho loves her.

Beatrice demands that Eddie leave the girl alone. She then advises Catherine to begin acting independently. She should realize that Eddie has never liked any boy she brought home. Bea also says that she must behave as if she were mature. She cannot hug Eddie the way she did as a child of twelve. Catherine sadly promises to be more discreet.

Eddie calls on Alfieri, contending that Rodolpho is courting Catherine to speed his way to naturalization. The lawyer replies that he has no proof. Eddie then suggests that the boy is odd or effeminate. He calls attention to the immigrant's slight build, blond hair, high voice, and creative talents. He even helped Catherine cut out a blouse. Alfieri again sees nothing illegal, except the unauthorized immigration. But Eddie denies that he would ever use this. He does say, however, that he has worked hard for too long to let such a worthless type rob him. Alfieri urges him to drop the matter, but Eddie is dissatisfied. The lawyer knows that there is tragedy ahead, but can do nothing to prevent it.

One evening, the family discuss the brothers' earlier fishing trips to Africa from Italy. Marco hopes to see his wife again in a few years. Eddie again criticizes Rodolpho for being too free with his niece. He not only keeps her out too long, but risks getting caught. In reply, Catherine invites Rodolpho to dance to a record they bought together. Marco tells Eddie that on one fishing trip his brother did the cooking. Eddie, harshly joking, says there is no place on the waterfront for men who sing and cook. He then insists upon teaching Rodolpho to box. The boy makes a brave attempt to learn, but Eddie gives him a sharp blow. Thereupon Rodolpho and Catherine resume their dance. Marco, finally aware of Eddie's enmity, challenges him to lift a heavy chair by grasping only one of its legs. Eddie cannot accomplish the feat but Marco handles it easily. Eddie now has a worthy opponent.

ACT II. Alfieri recalls that, right before Christmas, the longshoremen unloaded a case of whiskey with studied carelessness, then appropriated the bottles. At that time Catherine and Rodolpho were for once at home alone. Worried about Eddie's anger, she asks Rodolpho if they could live in Italy after marriage. He rules out the possibility. They would be too poor. Eddie, she says sadly, is now always disagreeable. Actually, she has always understood his moods better than Beatrice ever did. How can she now walk out, even if he is unfair? Rodolpho soothes her and leads her into the bedroom.

Arriving home intoxicated because of the stolen Scotch, Eddie is startled to find Catherine with her dress awry. When, however, Rodolpho emerges from the bedroom, Eddie orders him to pack his things and leave. Tearfully, Catherine says that then she too must go. This Eddie forbids. Then seizing Rodolpho, Eddie holds him in a mocking, shameful embrace. Catherine is horrified, and Eddie again warns Rodolpho to get out and not return.

Eddie visits Alfieri again after Christmas. Because Rodolpho did not break his grip during the contemptuous embrace, Eddie is more than ever certain that the youth cannot be virile. Yet Catherine is determined to marry him. Once more, Alfieri declares that he cannot legally halt the pair. He also warns him indirectly not to court the censure of all his neighbors by informing.

Undeterred, Eddie grimly calls the Immigration Office, and anonymously gives them his address. Arriving home, he finds Beatrice taking down holiday decorations. Marco and his brother have moved upstairs, and Beatrice is clearly resentful. Eddie tries to assert some authority, but she continues to argue. Finally, he agrees to let Catherine go out more and meet other boys. But his permission comes too late. Beatrice now asks only that he attend Catherine's wedding. Catherine herself, still smarting, reluctantly seconds the invitation. From her, Eddie learns that two new "submarines," relatives of Lipari the butcher, are sharing the upstairs quarters with Marco and Rodolpho. Horrified, he urges the women to get all the immigrants out fast. But even as they hesitate, government officials arrive. Over the protests of Catherine and Bea, they arrest the brothers and the new arrivals. As he is taken away, Marco spits at Eddie and accuses him of betrayal. Eddie denies this, but all those around him regard him with deep suspicion.

At the prison, Alfieri has bailed out Rodolpho so that he can marry Catherine and take out his papers. They want Marco at the wedding, but only if he will promise not to fight Eddie. Finally, he yields. Meanwhile, at home, Eddie forbids Beatrice to attend the ceremony. At length, she sadly surrenders, sending the embittered Catherine off with her blessing. Rodolpho comes and tries vainly to pacify Eddie. But Eddie demands an apology from Marco. Unable to keep his pledge to Alfieri, Marco appears, angrily reiterating his charges. They fight, and Eddie falls mortally wounded, as Bea sobs. Alfieri confesses that he cannot help secretly admiring this stubborn man. So few today will hold out so uncompromisingly for what they believe.

ANALYSES OF THE MAJOR CHARACTERS

EDDIE CARBONE: This decent, hard-working longshoreman

becomes a man of destiny when he stubbornly refuses to accept what he believes to be a plot against his niece. Actually, as Alfieri and Bea both try to suggest tactfully, he himself has developed an unfortunate emotional attachment for Catherine that induces him to misjudge the carefree young Rodolpho. He cannot, however, be made to see in time that he is wrong, and he is unwilling to compromise. So he takes a drastic step to prevent the marriage, one that brings about his own death.

Although Eddie's unacknowledged passion for Catherine gives rise to a jealous dislike of Rodolpho or of any other man showing interest in her, there are other aspects of Eddie's character that serve to aggravate this hostility. For one thing, Eddie has rather strict, old-world notions of decorum. He worries about the girl's short skirt and possibly "wavy" walk, before the cousins even arrive. He also insists upon his "respect," as head of the household. His consent must be won if Catherine is to take the job, and he is quite firm in forbidding Bea to attend the wedding. Hence, his complaint that Rodolpho has been too "free" in asking Catherine out without his permission, is not wholly a matter of unreasoning jealousy. Eddie obviously adheres to the stricter requirements of earlier European codes. Ironically, of course, the newcomer, Rodolpho, is ready to become quickly Americanized.

Secondly, Eddie has in his personality a curious cynical strain. He does, of course, steal coffee and liquor with others from the piers, and he is part of a fair-sized operation to smuggle in immigrants. Actually, the conspiratorial act itself does not seem to affect his conscience, for it is an "honor" for him to help those in distress. Yet in the background is the syndicate running the racket, who will assure a man of a job until his debt to them is paid. There is clearly little altruism or humanitarianism in this end of the business.

Basically, however, Eddie is cynical regarding the love avowals of others. He warns Catherine about all the neighborhood men, even his close friends, as well as the sailors and office workers she may meet if she takes the job. To some extent, such warnings again probably stem from his possessiveness toward her. Yet when Marco talks of faithful wives patiently waiting in Italy, Eddie is quick to make a sly witticism about children born out of wedlock. This remark has no obvious bearing on the relationship between his niece and Rodolpho, although he is probably being testier than usual. But Marco's slow, serious rejoinder does suggest that Eddie is much too prompt to suspect the worst. Hence, he easily convinces himself that Rodolpho might marry Catherine merely to get himself citizenship papers.

Thirdly, Eddie has a fairly high opinion of his own righteousness. For one thing, he sees himself as the admirable provider. Even when jobs were scarce, he scorned to rely on relief, but went to piers all over the area to hunt work. Because he is so proud of having worked hard over the years to support himself, his wife, and his wife's needy relatives, he is most unsympathetic when Rodolpho indulges in a mild spending spree. It is doubtful, of course, that anything the boy did would be likely to satisfy him, once Catherine's fondness for him was jealously noted. But Eddie is clearly not accustomed to lavish spending. Catherine's new skirt is an event, and Beatrice has no really presentable tablecloth and no extra food in the house. So Eddie would naturally be unimpressed with a youth, sheltered in his own home, who uses his first pay to buy modish clothes and a record.

In addition, he is conscious of his generosity. He has taken into his home and raised, as his own daughter, Catherine, who is his wife's niece. He has also been good to Beatrice's family on other occasions. They mention his giving up his bed when her father's house burned down. Now he is extending hospitality to two more of her relatives. He does not ask for thanks. To help those hard pressed is an "honor." But he is also a man who does not want to be "pushed around." So the thought that Rodolpho has taken some unfair advantage is particularly galling. And, of course, when Beatrice sides with the opposition, he is angered still further, remembering all he has done for her and her people.

Fifthly, he thinks of himself as a good husband and foster father. However cynical he may be as regards other men, he is appalled at the very idea that he might be showing an unseemly interest in his niece. There is, of course, no evidence that he ever attempts to seduce her or to lead her into some illicit affair. He merely tries to steer her away from even normal dating with boys, and becomes easily annoyed when she shows some preference for the young Rodolpho. Both Alfieri and Beatrice are aware that his passions are roused, but he reacts with fury at the very suggestion. No good man in his world could be guilty of incestuous tendencies. But he is certain of his own goodness. So the charge must be preposterous.

Finally, Eddie is very proud of his manliness. To be a respected man on the piers requires strength and vigor, and he sees himself as undeniably virile. At the same time, he has no use whatever for less masculine men. The slight, blond Rodolpho who can sing, cook, and sew, belongs, to his way of thinking, only in a dress shop. Waterfront workers must be made of sterner stuff. Again, his suppressed desire for Catherine assuredly leaves him disinclined to give the young Italian any benefit of the doubt. But his friends Louis and Mike, with no personal grievances, also appear somewhat contemptuous of the boy. So to some extent, Eddie is applying the standards of his group. That his own pride is involved, however, is brought out most clearly when Marco uses the chair-lifting feat to prove to him that someone can be huskier, and more of a man, than even he is.

It is therefore apparent that Eddie gets strong support for his prejudice from these other elements in his background and his personality. But however great his antagonism, he is not one to rush into violence. He consults the lawyer, Alfieri, twice, and makes various efforts to convince Catherine, before taking action. And even when he does move, in desperation, he does not wield a knife. He makes a phone call. He is, of course, aware of possible dire consequences. He knows what ostracism can mean in his world. But to avoid taking this crucial step would be to tolerate a monstrous injustice and to fail to shield his household. For all his wrongheadedness, Eddie has a certain heroic determination. And he defends his curious convictions to the death.

ALFIERI: This kindly, reflective middle-aged attorney regards his humble, uneducated clients with great understanding and sympathy. He listens patiently to problems, gives them friendly as well as strictly legal advice, and is tolerantly amused when they shy away from him on the street due to, in the old country, lawyers' meaning bad news.

He seems sincerely interested in upholding the law. He is certainly no clever moneymaker who takes advantage of Eddie's plight to engage in sharp practice and build up fees. He gives this troubled man, the son of an earlier client, common-sense counsel to put out of his mind a situation that no legal statute covers. At the same time, he obviously knows about the presence of the illegal "submarines," and does not feel called upon to turn informer. In fact, knowing that should Eddie place his call, he will be courting the penalties imposed upon traitors by any group, he does nothing to encourage this type of compliance.

Alfieri is a perceptive man. He is not unusually friendly with Eddie's family. Yet when Eddie comes to him, he quickly divines the real source of the difficulty. There is no indication that he ever takes Eddie's charges seriously. He sees instead that Eddie is unduly preoccupied with the young girl. He is also, however, tactful and considerate. He tries very gently to explain to the anxious Eddie that he must let Catherine follow her own course. He does not succeed, because Eddie is alarmed at the very notion that he might be guilty of any such irregularity and fights more stubbornly than ever to defend his view. But Alfieri at least has made amiable and intelligent efforts to help.

Alfieri is also a sensitive, thoughtful individual, who is keenly aware of how little he or the law can do under certain circumstances. He is all but certain that Eddie's misconception will lead to tragedy. He has all the necessary facts before him. But what can he do? No crime has yet been committed, with the exception of the illegal entry. And again with this one proviso, no one is breaking any law. He has the sad feeling of being powerless, and yet he is also fascinated.

Finally, the lawyer is something of a romantic. He is, of course, sensible enough to realize that Brooklyn is a better place to live in since the Al Capone gang and others have vanished. And as he grows older, he rather enjoys the peaceful atmosphere. The cases he handles are largely the small claims of the poor, but he is getting along all right. Then along comes a case like that of the uncompromising, unyielding Eddie. Here is something that recalls to Alfieri the more exciting, more dramatic epochs in Italian history. Eddie's intense concentration upon his dilemma is dangerous and destructive. But there is a sort of rare heroic wildness, now almost stamped out, that Alfieri cannot help almost guiltily admiring. Most of the time he is solidly in favor of civilization. But encountering an occasional Eddie Carbone, unreasonable and untamed, proves a curiously exhilarating experience.

CATHERINE: At seventeen, Catherine is not quite certain whether she is really a grown woman or still Eddie's little daughter. As the play progresses, she develops some independence. Bea, for one, makes her realize, although somewhat reluctantly, that she cannot go on behaving like an affectionate twelve-year-old with her possibly susceptible uncle. And Eddie himself has warned her that she must begin to conduct herself with new restraint or be judged to be like "all the girls." Rodolpho, of course, by taking her out and eventually proposing to her, helps her decide what she wants most out of life. And Eddie's persistent hostility and cruel attack on Rodolpho at last so alienate her that she has no further hesitation.

For all of Eddie's protective caution, Catherine is animated by the spirit of the New World rather than by that of the Old. She does recognize that she must get Eddie's consent to leave school and take the job. But her very enthusiasm about going out and making good wages is that of an enterprising young American. Again, she likes records, enjoys comic movies, and has a wonderful time on dates with Rodolpho. It is true that Catherine does not want to hurt Eddie. She knows that he has been good to her, and she is fond of him. But from the first she obviously finds his advice about being careful at least surprising. She is a sufficiently typical modern Brooklyn teenager to take freedom as her due and to look forward lightheartedly to making her own way.

Yet Catherine, for all her girlish innocence, has not, in fact, entirely discouraged Eddie's interest. She is greatly surprised when

Beatrice suggests that a wife might see cause for jealousy. Yet she does certainly, before the advent of Rodolpho, give Eddie almost worshipful attention. And at one point she reveals to Rodolpho a certain smug attitude toward Bea. Bea nags Eddie all the time instead of making him happy. She, Catherine, on the other hand, understands his moods and knows how to cheer him up when he is sad. So there has been, perhaps, some suppressed sense of rivalry. In general, however, Catherine is an exuberant youngster ready to enjoy life and genuinely desirous of keeping everybody happy. She is, of course, impatient. She wants the job as soon as possible, and she is equally eager to marry almost at once. For that matter, she does not resist Rodolpho's tender advances before the ceremony. Yet her warm feelings for Eddie are all but destroyed when he tries to shame Rodolpho. When he then forbids Bea to go to her wedding, she calls him a "rat" and defies him like a bitter, angry child. Yet the next minute, seeing the danger that threatens, she is once more anxiously pleading. To sum up, then, Catherine is a nice, reasonably normal girl caught up in an explosive situation. Thus, while she does little that is deliberately disruptive, she does play a very real part in Eddie's plunge toward disaster.

BEATRICE: A good, pious housewife, Beatrice tries hard to smooth over differences between her husband and her niece. She is no sophisticated Alfieri, but, like him, she shrewdly evaluates the situation. She warns Eddie that his concern is excessive, and she attempts to get Catherine to show both more prudence and firmer resolution. If Eddie strives to keep the girl a "baby," Bea works to make her grow up.

Bea, however, cannot succeed with Eddie. For one thing, she herself is anxious and unsure. She may suspect that Eddie's failure to make love to her during the past months is due to his worry over Catherine. But she is also uneasy lest she may have done something to lessen his affection. Her worried questions, far from getting her a helpful answer, embarrass Eddie and make a better relationship even less likely.

In addition, as Catherine once points out to Rodolpho, Bea tends to nag. She has excellent intentions, and she is often right in her arguments. But she does little to bolster her husband's self-confidence. By continually pointing out to him how wrong he is in his attitude, she puts him on the defensive, increases his stubbornness, and makes him regard her as lined up with those who are out to defeat him.

Toward the end, Bea finds herself terribly torn by conflicting loyalties. She is undoubtedly fond of Catherine and wants to give her a pleasant family wedding. She knows that Eddie's contemptu-

ous baiting of Rodolpho hurts her deeply, and she would like
to temper the girl's bitterness. Yet she never forgets that she is
Eddie's wife. And when the ultimatum is delivered, she will stay
home from the ceremony rather than jeopardize her own marriage.
She will also speak quite sharply to her angry niece, when the
girl starts calling Eddie unpleasant names. Despite her frantic
efforts, Bea cannot keep Eddie from meeting the now menacing
Marco, and Eddie falls mortally stabbed. Ironically, it is Bea,
not Catherine, whom he thinks of when dying. But this new
awareness comes too late to be of help to anyone.

RODOLPHO and **MARCO:**   The brothers offer startling con-
trasts. Rodolpho is blond, carefree, and artistic. Marco is a mature, concerned family man, slow-speaking and of great strength.
The boy, who dreams of owning a shiny motorcycle, sings his
heart out, laughs at American movie comedies, and falls happily
in love with the pretty Catherine. Marco is primarily preoccupied
with getting enough money sent overseas to provide for his wife
and children.

Rodolpho has every intention of being completely American. He
even sings an American popular song the first night, and he makes
it clear to Catherine that he has no desire to bring her back to
live in Italy. Marco, however, wants to rejoin his family. And
it becomes evident that this quiet but powerful man has much
of the Old World in his attitudes toward life.

Once having recognized Eddie's campaign against Rodolpho,
he comes to his brother's aid. The trick of lifting the chair is a
decisive warning to Eddie to leave the boy alone. Later, when
Eddie acts as informer, Marco's fury is frightening. Not only
has Eddie attacked his brother; he has now made it impossible
for Marco to aid his hungry children back in Italy.

Once roused, Marco is implacable. Alfieri tries to get him to keep
the peace if released, pending a hearing. And the lawyer insists
that he must leave whatever vengeance is due Eddie in God's
hands. But Marco, for all his anxiety to provide for his family,
cannot give a valid promise to avoid Eddie. Justice must be
done. If the law will not bring it about, then it is his solemn
duty to avenge the honor of his house. Decrying Eddie as an
"animal," he strikes him down, forcing Eddie's drawn knife back
into his foe's body.

Like Eddie, Marco still follows an ancient code, not wholly ap-
propriate for modern conditions. But also like Eddie, he does
not know the meaning of compromise. Whatever the cost, the
malefactor must be punished, the insult wiped out. In fact, he
comes to Eddie directly from the church. In his view, destroying
so barbarous an "animal" is a sacred obligation.

COMMENTARY ON *A VIEW FROM THE BRIDGE*

INITIAL REACTION. The earlier, shorter version of *A View from the Bridge* opened as part of a double bill with *A Memory of Two Mondays* in September, 1955. There were few enthusiastic notices, and the production ran for only four months. Miller thought the poor reception due partially to staging problems, yet he himself was not wholly satisfied with the development of *A View from the Bridge*. So he subsequently expanded it to a full-length play, which was well received in London. During the 1964-1965 season, this version was offered off-Broadway in New York. The reviews this time were most enthusiastic, and the work was hailed as a powerful, perceptive drama.

UNUSUAL MATERIAL. Hitherto Arthur Miller had written mainly of middle-class Americans with no obvious cultural link with a specific European country. The townspeople in *The Crucible* were by the 1690's, it is true, still English subjects; but only the exotic Barbados come up for mention, not the mother country. In *A View from the Bridge,* however, Miller deals with Americans who retain strong ties with Italy, the land of their ancestors. Not only do they help Italian relatives enter this country illegally. Many of their standards and values, as regards, for instance, the father's position in the home and the obligation to avenge insults to one's family, derive from an older European code. In addition, the longshoreman's family, as Brooklyn tenement dwellers, are in somewhat humbler circumstances than the Kellers of *All My Sons* or even the Lomans of *Death of a Salesman*.

SENSATIONAL ELEMENT. If the ethnic group described seemed not in Miller's usual province, two themes in the work suggested to some that the playwright had decided to try more sensational material. For one thing, there was the question of incest. Eddie Carbone is shown to be unduly fond of his wife's niece, Catherine. In addition, there is the subject of perversion. Eddie insists to the lawyer Alfieri that Rodolpho is "not right," and hence could not make Catherine a suitable husband. When no one believes him, he subjects the young man to a mocking embrace to humiliate him before Catherine.

Actually, neither theme is handled in particularly shocking fashion. Catherine is, after all, not Eddie's daughter, but the niece of his wife; even though Eddie has brought her up as his own, she is not a close blood relative of the type usually considered in stories of incest. In addition, their relationship involves no overtly improper acts. Catherine is basically a normal young girl, who wants only to marry the handsome young Rodolpho. And Eddie, whatever his unconscious drives, thinks of himself as merely doing his fatherly duty in attempting to stop her from marrying someone who could not possibly make her a good husband. Eddie is in fact horrified when Alfieri suggests that there is some personal jealousy involved in his hostility toward Rodolpho.

As for the perversion charge, it is made reasonably clear that this is merely Eddie's way of attempting to defeat a rival for Catherine's devotion. The accusation itself reveals much regarding Eddie's habits of thought and characteristic attitudes. But Alfieri, the sensible, educated "chorus," refuses to see in it anything more than a cloak for Eddie's frustrated passion. And Rodolpho acts throughout as a good-natured youth interested in marrying Catherine.

CULTURAL CONFLICTS. One area in which the playwright shows considerable interest is that of opposing cultural norms or standards. Regardless of his inner feelings regarding Catherine, Eddie has Old World ideas as to how a young girl should be shielded and protected, and how courtships should be handled. Catherine, on the other hand, is an American teen-ager eager to take a job and earn money of her own and also to go out freely to see a film or take a walk with a boy she likes. The older Bea, on the other hand, although she sometimes argues with Eddie, pays due heed to him as head of the house.

There are also interestingly varied attitudes concerning the illegal immigrants. Eddie and his family are essentially decent, hard-working people, hardly criminals in the usual sense. Yet, to help poor Italian relatives come to this country to get work, they think it only honorable to help violate immigration laws. Moreover, it might normally be an admirable action to call to the attention of the authorities some flagrant offense against the law. Here, however, the informer is the worst of traitors, to be ostracized for the rest of his life with scorn and contempt. It is curious to see how Miller has his educated and compassionate Alfieri view this situation. Understanding his clients, Alfieri makes no move to interfere with the smuggling in of aliens, which he knows is going on. At the same time, he will not counsel anyone to break the law, and makes every effort to secure Marco's pledge to take no violent action before securing his release. In the long run, however, both Marco and Eddie put personal and family claims ahead of community claims, just as they had put the latter before that of the American law. Eddie turns informer ostensibly to protect his immediate household. Marco fights to avenge his brother's honor and his own.

MODERN TRAGEDY. Because of the incest motif, the loves and hates within the family, and the final violent clash, as well as the choric function of Alfieri, some critics have pointed out parallels between A View from the Bridge and the ancient Greek tragedies. It is also clear, however, that the work is in line with the concept of modern tragedy presented in such earlier Miller works as *Death of a Salesman*. Again the hero is a contemporary "common man," completely devoid of the wealth and influence of the traditional protagonist. Eddie lives in a tenement and works on the docks. In addition, the hero's goals are hardly impressive objectively. He does not seek great conquests or lasting fame. He merely wants to stop an adopted daughter from marrying a young immigrant. Yet, like previous Miller heroes, he, too, gives "full commitment" to his unfortunate convictions. His thinking may sometimes make little more sense than that of Willy Loman. But once he is certain, however unreasonably, that he is right, he will sacrifice everything for his beliefs. He is clearly aware of what his people think of informers. Even if Marco never kills him, he is giving up his status in the community. But he cannot do otherwise. And it is in this passionate refusal to compromise that Alfieri and presumably Miller perceive the heroic quality of the troubled, wrong-headed Eddie.

TECHNIQUE. Much comment has centered on the use of Alfieri, the lawyer, as chorus. The idea seems to have been that since Eddie and his people could not have been articulate enough to explore the ironies and ambiguities of their situation involving cultural conflicts, Alfieri could serve as compassionate interpreter. Some have thought that the character adds dimension to the work; others have questioned the need for such a role. Incidentally, in the published version of *The Crucible*, Miller includes explanatory comments throughout. These interpretive remarks were read by an actor standing to one side, in at least one off-Broadway revival of the play, but were not included in a subsequent production.

A second technical feature of *A View from the Bridge* was the use of a sort of free verse form in certain of the lines, especially Alfieri's. There were also poetic lines in *A Memory of Two Mondays*. In general, however, Miller, in working out the longer version of Eddie's story, reverted largely to prose.

Finally, the title has interested some writers. The bridge can literally be, of course, Brooklyn Bridge, suggesting the waterfront area where Eddie works. But there is also probably some symbolism intended. Is Alfieri himself, perhaps, on the bridge between Old World and New, between the heroic society of powerful, unleashed passions and the modern era, in which civilized controls encourage compromise?

REVIEW QUESTIONS AND ANSWERS

1. Eddie's hostility to Rodolpho seems to derive mainly from

Eddie's frustrated passion for Catherine. Does Arthur Miller, however, also suggest other contributory factors?

ANSWER: To appreciate fully Eddie's dislike of Rodolpho, Eddie's background must be taken into account. First of all, Eddie is a hard-working man who has had to struggle to support his family, especially during Depression years. Hence, he has no use for a carefree young man who will "waste" his first earnings on a record and rather flashy clothes. Secondly, Eddie's life experiences and circle of acquaintances have been relatively limited. His friends are all burly, strong, rather close-mouthed dock workers like himself. They have always been his classic examples of how manly men look and behave. Rodolpho does not fit the pattern. He is a slight youth, artistically inclined and given to bursting into song. Hence it is easy for Eddie to question his virility.

In addition, Eddie's involvement in violation of laws has left him skeptical and wary. His warnings to the women, early in the play, to observe strict silence, indicate how uncertain he is of others. At the same time, he is always somewhat afraid that others may take advantage of his generosity. Half-jokingly, he tells Beatrice he does not want to be deprived of his own bed. So it is not unlikely that this guarded, somewhat cynical man might suspect that Rodolpho was using Catherine to obtain citizenship papers more readily.

Finally, there is the element of chance, or mischance. Eddie, intoxicated, happens to come home just when the two young lovers have been there alone for the first time. Even a less hostile father and host might find the picture disturbing. To Eddie it is the culminating proof of Rodolpho's perfidy.

2. In setting the scene, Alfieri talks of earlier years in the same Brooklyn area, when violent crimes were more frequent. Would Miller have made his work more effective by having his story take place during that more turbulent period?

ANSWER: Most of Miller's plays involve violence. Ed Keller and Willy Loman commit suicide, as does Maggie apparently in *After The Fall*. And most of the admirable characters in *The Crucible* are hanged. In general, however, the playwright is concerned with the type of passionate upholding of some personal ideal that is most startling when it turns up amidst the very ordinary surroundings of a fairly commonplace group.

First of all, such a situation makes possible an element of effective dramatic contrast. In *Death of a Salesman*, for instance, the neighbor, Charley, who drops over to play cards, suggests a whole society of modest, easy-going people very different from the agonized, wildly aspiring Willy. And the little neighborhood group that chat of Sunday papers in Ed Keller's backyard in *All My Sons* set off strikingly the bitter father-and-son clash that will drive the genial Ed to suicide. So, too, the generally nonviolent atmosphere of Eddie Carbone's Brooklyn makes Eddie's stubborn one-man campaign seem more theatrically impressive.

Moreover, although Arthur Miller has insisted that heroes can emerge from middle- or lower-class modern groups, he still views the hero as an exceptional individual. As a character he may not be more intelligent than others—he may, in fact, as here, be sadly deluded. But he does pursue his vision more ardently than those around him, even at the cost of all else that he holds dear. Hence, were Eddie merely one more violent man in a violent society, his acts would probably not seem at all heroic in this sense.

3. Do Beatrice and Catherine contribute in any way to Eddie's catastrophe?

ANSWER: At first glance, Beatrice would seem to be merely one more innocent bystander caught up in an unfortunate situation. Certainly, she is a good woman and a faithful, conscientious wife. She cares about her husband and wants to be pleasing to him. Even when she is irked over his treatment of Catherine and Rodolpho, she stops the girl from calling Eddie names. She also accepts eventually, although with sadness, Eddie's order that she remain away from the wedding. Yet, according to Catherine, she nags Eddie too much. In this instance it is clear that she does see his possessive attitude toward Catherine and tries to warn him against it. But she is not one to lavish affectionate praise. Indeed, there is some indication that Eddie turns to the young, enthusiastic Catherine because she makes a fuss over him, whereas Beatrice, decent and good-hearted as she is, is more apt to hand out advice. Eddie throughout worries about not receiving his due "respect." Beatrice, apparently, is not able to make him feel emotionally secure. Hence, he is drawn to Catherine, and trouble ensues.

For her part, Catherine is young, innocent, and genuinely fond of Eddie. She is not "in love" with him. It is Rodolpho whom she wants to marry. Yet, from what Bea says and from what Catherine herself tells Rodolpho, it is evident that the girl has, even if unintentionally, acted in a way to rouse Eddie's masculine interest. She has been rather casual about appearing only partially dressed in his presence. And she has behaved toward him with the sort of affection proper to a small child. She is also proud about recognizing his moods and knowing when he wants a beer. She is a nice, quite normal young girl, but she has not been above taking over certain of Bea's wifely ministrations.

AFTER THE FALL

(1964)

CHARACTERS

QUENTIN. A sensitive, introspective lawyer in his forties, painfully aware that he has often failed to live up to his own ideals, and pondering whether he can still build a satisfactory future.

FELICE. A bright, effervescent young client, grateful to Quentin for obtaining her divorce and for his taking a friendly personal interest in her and her problems.

MAGGIE. Quentin's second wife, a beautiful blond entertainer, sometimes childlike and wistful, sometimes bitter, coarse and sensual.

HOLGA. A young German archaeologist, whom Quentin admires; a strong, compassionate survivor of Nazi horrors, who knows the worst that man can do and still has hope.

DAN. Quentin's older brother, who goes into the family business and does not begrudge young Quentin his chance for a college education.

FATHER. A businessman for whom Quentin had little respect, thanks to his mother's scathing denunciations.

MOTHER. A disillusioned woman, regretting her marriage to an uneducated man who has failed in business, and determined to get what is due her by having her son, Quentin, succeed brilliantly.

ELSIE. The cultivated, esteemed wife of Quentin's friend, Lou, who shocks Quentin both with her casual immodesty and with her cowardly reluctance to let her husband publish his new textbook.

LOUISE. Quentin's first wife, a capable homemaker, distressed and angry because Quentin seems aloof and unresponsive when she craves attention.

LOU. Quentin's friend and former law professor, now under investigation because of his earlier association with radical movements.

MICKEY. A member of Quentin's law firm, also under investigation for radicalism, who decides to tell everything and name names to the Committee.

OTHER CHARACTERS. Minor figures turn up briefly now and then. Several are associated with Maggie. There is the man in the park who flirts with her; and there are her dresser, Carrie, and her designer, Lucas, who help arrange her wedding dress. Also in view on occasion are her secretary and her pianist. Two other characters are introduced in a short scene showing the investigating committee in action. They are the insistent Chairman and one Harley Barnes, a minister questioned about Communist affiliations. There are also hospital nurses caring for Quentin's father, a porter, and those representing the general public at airports or in cafes.

SETTING

The action is said to occur in Quentin's mind. The set, constructed with three levels, the loftiest at the rear, suggests specific locations only vaguely, except, perhaps, for the ruined concentration-camp tower seen in the background. As Quentin recalls past episodes or remembers people who influenced him, figures appear and vanish, sometmes silently, sometimes pausing to re-enact scenes. Lighting is used skillfully for fluid effects.

PLOT ANALYSIS

ACT I. Quentin, a genial but troubled lawyer in his forties, has dropped in to talk over a crucial decision with an unseen Listener. During the year following the death of Maggie, his second wife, Quentin has given up his law work and lived quietly. Four months ago his mother also died, while he was traveling abroad. At that time he found himself attracted to Holga, a young German archaeologist. But after two unhappy marriages, he hesitates about a third. Holga is now flying to New York for a meeting. Should he welcome her and try to make a new start?

He is encouraged by the memory of Felice, an enthusiastic young divorce client who idolizes him. But he is soon disheartened by other memories of the tragic Maggie and his now dead mother. He relives the scene when, summoned home by his brother Dan, he bluntly broke the news of their mother's death to his father, still weak from an operation. The old man was shocked, but took things in stride. Pondering this curious hardness in people, Quentin is soon mentally back with Holga, visiting a ruined Nazi concentration camp. Even there she is cheerful and loving, but he is uneasy, fearing he might some day break faith with her. She reassures him, for, after all, she has not been above reproach. She was slow to defy the Nazis. He is relieved that she is not wholly certain. Yet he wishes he had beliefs as strong as those held by the Nazis. He has only doubts.

He cannot seem to mourn his mother. He remembers how she urged him as a small boy to improve his handwriting. In doing so she sneers at his father as an ignorant man whom she regrets having forgone college to marry. At this point Father joins them, admitting sadly that his business has failed even though he cashed in all their insurance and securities to bolster it. Mother furiously denounces him as a fool, to young Quentin's dismay. Back in Germany, Quentin wonders how Holga can seem serene despite her knowledge of Nazi atrocities. She says that one must accept his own life, however deplorable, just as a true mother might kiss an unappealing idiot child. He misses Holga, but still fears to commit himself to new promises.

His mind reverts to earlier years with his first wife, Louise, when values seemed more stable. How disturbed he was then when Elsie, the wife of Lou, his admired law professor, behaved without due modesty. He sees again the kindly Lou praising a brief of his but worried about being subpoenaed to testify about past radical associations. Lou admits he did formerly lie to help the Communist Party he now rejects. Elsie scornfully warns him not to stir up new inquiries by publishing his just completed textbook. Her contempt reminds Quentin of his mother's scathing words to his father.

In his next memory, he and Louise, married seven years, are drifting apart. She accuses him of failing to pay her sufficient notice. Reading her his briefs is not enough. He feels guilty, knowing that he was never wholly unaware of other attractive women. Had he then some element in him of the betrayal guilt that built Nazi camps? He cannot forget how his mother used him, her literary son, as a subtle weapon against her uneducated husband.

Quentin now recalls a bitter exchange between Lou and Mickey, another old friend and fellow lawyer. Also called to testify about past leftist ties, Mickey plans to tell all and name names. Quentin thinks this unwise, and Lou accuses him of turning informer to save his own property. Their pleasant relationship is at an end.

Sometime later Lou has been accused, presumably after Mickey testified, and Quentin loyally but reluctantly is handling his defense. Louise, meanwhile, has gone into psychoanalysis. She accuses Quentin of talking her down at social gatherings and of showing less interest in her than in other women. He counters that she is cold and unresponsive, but she accuses him of expecting continual praise. And she is not his mother! He notes that he is defending Lou, because old ties count and he cannot be a "separate" person thinking only of himself. Louise says that he is immature and calls him an idiot.

Then on a park bench he meets Maggie, the beautiful little blonde chatterbox who runs his office switchboard. They talk lightly of lost dogs, discount records and her former job as a beauty products demonstrator. He finds her charming but worries about her accepting too freely the attentions of male admirers. He would have her fix her torn dress and be careful. Having discouraged some unsavory types from making further advances, he sends her home in a cab.

Coming in late, feeling virtuous and also strangely affectionate toward Louise, Quentin discovers that he has missed two meetings, one of parents at his daughter Betty's school, and the other of board members of his law firm. He tells Louise about Maggie, and she, hurt and angry, excludes him from their bedroom. Then suddenly he learns by phone that Lou has jumped or fallen to his death before a subway train. Quentin feels guilty, for even he, Lou's one remaining friend, could not hide his distaste for so unpopular a cause. And perhaps Lou's sense of being wholly deserted prompted his suicide. Yet Quentin must admit a certain relief, and he sees how decent tradesmen could help build death camps.

His marriage with Louise is over. He still cannot believe that there was to be no saving final reconciliation. Again he thinks of Holga, and of how curiously hopeful he still feels upon arising each morning. But he remembers too his agonizing experiences with Maggie.

ACT II. Eager for Holga's arrival, Quentin sadly remembers Maggie's breathtaking beauty on their wedding day and is afraid of killing still another woman's love. Felice, Mother, Maggie, and even Holga have been disconcertingly inclined to idolize him. His mother, for instance, envisioned for him a brilliant future that would decisively show up his failure of a father. She did, however, save him from being trapped in the family business; and his brother, Dan, kindly encouraged him to get the college education he had had to forgo.

A few years after the break with Louise, Quentin calls on Maggie, now a well-known singer of hit records. She thanks him for having once shown her sympathy and respect. Her own father rejected her. Quentin is like a god. Despite her success, she is frightened and lonely, sometimes having terrifying dreams of the guilty but fanatical mother who tried to kill her. Glad that Maggie is not too innocent, Quentin praises her for living the truth. Thinking back, however, he now is sure that he enjoyed believing he had the power to change her, as he had, in a small way, changed Felice.

He recalls another childhood betrayal. He was left home with the maid while his mother and the rest slipped off to Atlantic City. He locked himself in the bathroom and turned on the water ominously. Meeting Maggie again in the park, he is touched by her generous offer of love without marriage. He sees, however, that he must save her from agents who exploit her and even from predatory fans.

Or even then, he later wonders, was he living a lie? Where was the real Quentin?

He recalls defending Harley Barnes, a clergyman accused of Red leanings. The Committee accusers he found hypocritical, but Barnes in turn seemed too negative. Quentin thinks we must finally say something positive.

As his radiant, hopeful bride, Maggie thanks Quentin for saving her. She confesses more sordid past actions, but he says that her sufferings have made him understanding. Suddenly skeptical, she asks coarsely why he had to kiss Elsie so ardently.

Once married, Maggie redecorates extravagantly, insisting that they live for the present only. She becomes irritable and highhanded as a singer. Quentin takes over her law work but fails to please her. She complains about his mother and rebuffs him crudely.

She becomes an alcoholic and takes drugs. Appalled when she tries suicide, Quentin cannot leave her, remembering the abandoned Lou. Yet eventually he declares she must save herself or accept hospital care. He must finally act as a separate person, not being a God to love without limit. He begs her to admit her lies and cruelties, and he will confess his concealed hatreds. Bitterly she reminds him that he once wrote that he loved only his daughter and wanted to die. He did so on impulse, he replies, one night when he wondered which of their guests had been her lovers. She pleads again for his love, but he is certain that she wants only his destruction. While struggling to take the death-dealing drugs from her, he almost kills her. Or was he trying really to slay his mother?

Maggie dies at last, and again the grieving Quentin is curiously relieved. He thus resembles all who survived concentration camps, grateful that they were not the ones to die. Holga, however, knows that no one now is innocent. We live not in Eden, but after the Fall of Man. So with her, facing past and future with courage, he may have a chance.

ANALYSES OF THE MAJOR CHARACTERS

QUENTIN: This genial, troubled, highly self-conscious attorney here pleads and judges his own life case. He has, in effect, entered a petition to marry for the third time. The question is, can he regard himself as morally justified in taking such a step? His two previous unions ended unhappily, but he now finds himself attracted to a loving, sensible young German woman. Is he likely to ruin her life if he makes her his wife? What type of man is he? How responsible is he for certain past painful episodes? He searches his memory and proceeds to evaluate the evidence.

Essentially Quentin must determine the relative importance of outward conduct and interior, often largely suppressed, impulses. If he concentrates, for instance, on his actual behavior toward others, he measures up rather well. When married to Louise, he was a good provider and never had affairs with other women. When the accused Lou was deserted by old friends, Quentin took his case. When he married Maggie, he allowed her to follow her decorating whims, gave up his own work to manage her tangled business interests, accepted her arbitrary demands with extraordinary patience, and for a long time saw her through her suicidal bouts with drink and drugs. He came home at his brother's summons and broke the sad news of his mother's passing to his hospitalized father. He was kind and helpful to the young client, Felice, without taking advantage of her gratitude. And he has been fair with Holga, making her no glib promises while he is still unsure.

Since all this is true, it is hard for him to understand how he could have failed so conspicuously as a husband. It is, in fact, almost as hard to comprehend as is the atrocity record of the concentration camp. How could he, Quentin, a good man, cause misery to others? How could other presumably good men cooperate to inflict torture upon their fellow human beings?

When, however, he searches his heart further, he is aware of feelings and attitudes rather surprising in a virtuous individual. Even though he was not unfaithful to Louise in act, he did have desires to love other women. He may, in fact, have been the husband above reproach largely through cowardice. Again, since he always confided in Louise his interest in other women, he may have been seeking, as she testily suggests, fulsome praise for being such a paragon. As for Lou, he must admit that actually he was most reluctant to risk his reputation in defense of his suddenly unpopular friend. And he knows that Lou's untimely death left him almost inhumanly relieved. He would no longer have to face general disapproval.

Even his willingness to assume the unwelcome task of informing his father of his mother's death cannot pass too close scrutiny. For one thing, thanks to his mother's well-directed slurs against her husband over the years, Quentin had little respect left for his father. So he was not likely to worry so much about his feelings as did his concerned brother, Dan. For another, he has long felt unacknowledged deep resentment for his mother. She destroyed his regard for his father and used him selfishly as a weapon against her husband. She betrayed him by running off for the trip to Atlantic City. On the one hand she set for him impossibly high standards; on the other, in abusing his father, she somehow made him feel guilty. He hears her accusing tones when Elsie treats Lou with contempt, and when Louise berates him. And when in a moment of fury he reaches for Maggie's throat, he is suddenly aware of an impulse to choke his mother.

Even his relationship with Maggie has its dubious side. Maggie from the first was clearly far from conventional in her love life. When Quentin met her she may have appeared sweet and guileless, but she unashamedly admits having had an illicit affair with a married judge. And she is very free in her behavior toward park strangers. At first Quentin tries to ignore such disturbing signs or pay them little heed. Later he gets carried away with the idea of "saving" her. He tells himself that the past is unimportant and that her hard life has ruled out any censure on his part. He is not ashamed of her and is prepared to be her tower of strength. The only difficulty is that in reality he does mind greatly that her life has been so irregular. His attitude of benign indifference is essentially a pose. At almost their first party he wonders about her past relations with some of their guests and is wretched enough to think of suicide. This deep bitterness grows as she shows increasingly the less lovely sides of her personality; and for all his devoted care of her during her alcoholic bouts, he sees her more and more as a force driving him to destruction. Still generally the "good husband," he wants now only to free himself; and her eventual tragic death again seems the removal of a burden. The idea of saving her, which he identified with pure love, may have been primarily the urge to prove once more his moral superiority, whereas all the while he had within him hidden hatreds that would eventually bring him to the brink of murder.

Which then is the true Quentin—the good husband, or the would-be Lothario hesitating partly out of cowardice, partly out of smug self-righteousness? The faithful son fulfilling his proud mother's high hopes, or the bitter, hate-filled grown child of a vindictive traitress? The patient, selfless, almost fatherly guardian of a sick, pathetic little victim of society, or a hostile, resentful, insulted captive, wanting only escape and capable of murderous fury?

Thinking over these possibilities, Quentin finally concludes that it is not a clear "either-or" alternative. He has been, generally, a good son, a good husband, and a good friend. But not always. He must face the hard truth that he has also had mean or selfish tendencies, and that he has not always met his own lofty standards. His mother always filled him with ideas of being somebody special. Felice thought him magnificent, and Maggie saw him as a god. He was perhaps too ready to accept such high-flown characterizations, and was then too shocked when he failed to live up to expectations, theirs and his own. He nows sees that even normally decent men could have somehow built the concentration camps. After all, he was a good man and he came close to murder.

As for the future, he will go to Holga newly aware of his potential for evil, but hopeful that with her he will be able to recognize and control the less worthy impulses. He has come to terms with the "idiot child" that is his past. He has learned from it that he cannot say with certainty how he will act under any future combination of circumstances. But at least he will have fewer illusions about himself and thus will be able to face, more squarely, possible weaknesses. In reliving his past, Quentin thus gains in self-knowledge, and prepares to start anew without any total certainty, but with courage and some hope.

MAGGIE: This wistful, fragile-looking blonde is represented throughout as an immature, unstable personality, talented but woefully unsure of herself. In many ways she is a child hopelessly incapable of coping with adult problems in an adult way.

Much of her charm and winsome appeal is that of the child. Her chatter sparkles with youthful enthusiasm for lost dogs, new records, and her own lovely, unbroken hair. She can also be guilelessly trusting. She does not apparently attribute any dubious motives to men accosting her in the park, and she is very casual about willing everything to a possibly grasping agent. After a few kindly words from Quentin, she enshrines him as an idol; and she later cites her voice teacher as if he too were some godlike oracle. Even her generosity is that of an unsophisticated youngster. Her offer to provide a haven for Quentin without demanding marriage is an impulsive gesture but hardly a realistic solution.

She also seems often to experience the terrors of a child who is pathetically lonely and insecure. Rejected by her father, she cowers in her apartment bedroom, still conjuring up frightening visions of the mother who once tried to kill her. Even as she marries Quentin, who seems to promise some stability, she is fearfully blurting out details of past lapses to be sure he really wants to make her his wife. Later, when she is behaving with high-handed unreasonableness toward her business associates, she is actually afraid that they are all out to persecute and cheat her. Even her vulgar talk has in it something of a bewildered child's unruly defiance. And finally, she is apparently plunged into a kind of despair by coming across Quentin's scrawled assertion that he loves his daughter best.

In the climactic scene toward the end, Quentin tries to make her save herself by facing the facts of her life squarely and, in effect, growing up. This would mean that she would have to give up living exclusively in the present and stop airily refusing to worry about future bills. She would also have to admit her responsibility for certain past difficulties, and stop trying to place all the blame on parents, accompanists, or her husband. Finally, she would have to accept or, perhaps, try to remedy unfortunate situations, and not abandon all hope and drug herself senseless. Maggie, however, cannot heed his well-meant counsel. Feeling completely at bay, abandoned and abused by everyone, she bitterly refuses to swerve from her destructive course and dies from an overdose of barbiturates. By contrast, Quentin does, in general, follow his own prescription and goes on to live with at least moderate confidence.

LOUISE: This conscientious housewife gradually becomes dissatisfied with the insufficiently demonstrative Quentin. Unlike the more intellectual Elsie, she is not much interested in law work. Listening to Quentin's masterly brief is no treat for her, and she certainly cannot see in the fact that he read it to her any reassurance as to his interest in her personally. She wants to be noticed more, heard more attentively, and more often praised.

It is clear from the play that Quentin has, in fact, come to take her somewhat for granted. He is surprised and rather puzzled by her attitude, and amazed at his friend's suggestion that he try treating his wife as an interesting stranger whom he has just met.

The more offended Louise feels, however, the less she is able to secure the admiration she craves. For one thing, her accusing tone makes Quentin uneasy and defensive, rather than anxious to please. For another, having gone into psychoanalysis, she suddenly becomes very assertive at parties, determined to dominate discussions. Sensing that this is a challenge, Quentin takes the play away from her, and she is left more resentful than ever.

In addition, as her pride seems more and more offended, she becomes harder and more critical. When Quentin thoughtlessly misses a meeting and mentions his chance meeting with Maggie, she turns on him with suspicion and distrust. She even insists that he spend the night in the living-room despite his protests that such an arrangement would cause distress to their young daughter. Quentin unquestionably talks too much to his annoyed wife about other women he has sporadically admired. He regards himself as merely being honest and fair, and is rather smug about his good conduct. She is shrewd enough to recognize his thinly disguised appeal for approval, but accuses him of wanting her as mother, not as wife.

As the play describes the over-all situation, Quentin has no wish to break with his first wife. He likes being a well-established individual with a house, a wife, and a child. Yet her complaints, however legitimate, are delivered with such uncompromising sharpness that he cannot respond placatingly enough. Up to the end he hopes for some reconciliation. But both have their pride. And being unwilling to overlook minor irritations and to adopt a softer, more conciliatory approach, Louise, the good housewife, calls a halt to her marriage with Quentin.

HOLGA: This sensitive, considerate young German archaeologist appears to Quentin a much more serene, less demanding individual than the three women who previously affected his life. She does not make unreasonable demands as did his mother, she does not nag at him as Louise did, and she does not seem likely to cast upon him so many responsibilities as was Maggie's wont. Having lived in Germany during the Nazi eras, she has known some of the worst horrors of our generation, even lived in their midst. Yet she has remained calm and hopeful, and can still enjoy a music festival or some colorful wild flowers. She has her work and can exist as an independent person. She is fond of Quentin but will not hold him back should he feel the need to be free.

She bravely opposed the Nazi atrocities until captured and imprisoned. For this Quentin admires her, for he himself is an idealist. At the same time, he fears lest she be so strong and so noble that he might forever be left feeling by contrast guilty and inadequate. She, however, quickly assures him that she by no means feels wholly guiltless. Before she joined the underground movement, she did, after all, support her country perhaps longer than she should have. And were any of those who survived the Nazi injustices completely without blame? She does not pretend to know all the answers. She has merely come to accept her life for what it has been. And her combination of doubt and qualified optimism proves most heartening to Quentin, who for so long has vainly sought all-encompassing answers.

Holga, thus, loves and hopes. Sometimes sad, she is on the whole cheerful and resilient. She thus brings to the discouraged, puzzled Quentin the positive help he needs to start his life anew.

COMMENTARY ON *AFTER THE FALL*

CONTROVERSIAL WORK. The opening of *After the Fall* in January, 1964 was regarded well in advance as a major theatrical event. This was the first new work by Arthur Miller in over a decade, and there was much speculation as to whether or not he would equal or surpass his *Death of a Salesman*, first produced back in 1949. Also heightening interest was the advance word that the play was startlingly autobiographical and that Miller was working closely with those engaged in the production. Finally, this presentation had been chosen to launch the new Lincoln Center Repertory in the new, modern American National Theatre and Academy (ANTA) Theatre, near Washington Square, in New York City.

When the drama had its premiere, however, the critical response generally indicated only qualified approval. The production itself received high praise. The noted actor Jason Robards, Jr. was lauded for carrying off effectively the long and demanding role of Quentin. And a young newcomer, Barbara Loden, was universally acclaimed for her electrifying performance as the tormented Maggie. Since the play's action is said to occur in the hero's mind, there was need of special techniques for setting and over-all direction. Most commended the bare, vaulty, functional set and admired the swift, fluid, dramatic movement secured by director Elia Kazan.

AUTOBIOGRAPHICAL ELEMENT. Both critics and nonprofessional viewers, however, tended to focus their attention upon the unmistakable autobiographical content. Quentin may be a lawyer, not a playwright like Miller. But both are sensitive intellectuals, of middle years, liberal in political outlook. Both have had some experiences connected with Congressional investigating committees. Both, after having been twice divorced, select as third bride a young European woman. Miller, in fact, dedicates *After the Fall* to his wife, Ingeborg Morath.

What caused the greatest sensation, however, were the scenes dealing with the unstable Maggie. Arthur Miller's second wife was the beautiful blond film star, Marilyn Monroe, who eventually died an apparent suicide. Maggie, Quentin's second wife, is a highly paid popular singer who dies from excessive use of barbiturates. Barbara Loden, who created the role on the stage, seemed to many to resemble uncannily the late Miss Monroe. Some felt that in view of the obvious parallels, the vivid accounts of Maggie's violent, drunken outbursts were in questionable taste. Others were frankly fascinated, relishing what seemed the chance to listen in on the frank, intimate exchanges of a famous couple. Still others, professedly indifferent to possible real-life associations, considered the scenes noteworthy examples of lively, explosive dramatic writing.

In any event, the impression created was that the entire work focused upon some rather shocking aspects of Quentin's second marriage. Actually the play is much more complex. There are the significant childhood episodes and those related to the Congressional hearings. Then, too, there are substantial sections dealing with Louise, Holga, and even the minor figures, Lou, Elsie, and Felice. Above all, there is the central question of Quentin's coming to terms with not only his own anxiety-ridden past, but with the great cruelties and betrayals in his own native country and abroad.

Even when, however, the play was taken as a whole, certain criticisms were voiced. Some were prepared to concede that Miller as a serious writer was expressing candidly his thinking on issues vital to him personally. But even while acknowledging the skilled playing of Robards, they failed to find Quentin a truly interesting person. In addition, they doubted that Quentin was actually representative enough to be regarded as an "Everyman" figure or a typical man of our time. In addition, the form that Quentin's basic problem assumed seemed to some regrettably reminiscent of sentimental fiction. And they were not unduly concerned over whether or not a sensitive, middle-aged lawyer could find happiness in a contemplated third marriage.

Curiously enough, a more strongly favorable critical reaction seemed to develop outside New York following the publication of the play. Perhaps, in some ways, a truer perspective was achieved by those who missed the dynamic handling of the Maggie scenes by Robards and Barbara Loden. Whatever the cause, these subsequent comments did tend to discuss more Miller's outlook here on the nature of man, the problem of evil, and various moral and psychological issues of this era.

POLITICAL BACKGROUND. In the previous notes on *The Crucible,* reference was made to the national controversy over the work of Congressional investigation committees and to Miller's own related experiences. Here Quentin is pictured not as being under fire for past activities but merely as the sympathetic friend of two who have been subpoenaed.

Among the interesting aspects of the situation which Miller develops here is the dismay and agonized soul-searching of those suddenly called upon to justify past views and actions. Lou, for instance, is not at all proud of the compromises he made with his own scholarly integrity during the period when he favored Communism. Now publicly accused, he is not sure how he can explain deceptions that once seemed to him advisable. Mickey, too, feels distressed and guilty. He wants only to bare his soul, naming whatever names the Committee requests. In this way, he feels, he may get back not only his good reputation but his own self-respect. Quentin advises against such indiscriminate revelations, which he believes Mickey may later regret. Lou angrily accuses Mickey of betraying him and his other friends merely to save his own neck.

Quentin himself has no apologies for whatever radical leanings he once held. "We only turned left because it seemed the truth was there." As a gesture of friendship and loyalty, he agrees to take the case of the accused Lou. But he is not happy over the whole business. He thus, somewhat guiltily, feels considerable relief when Lou falls to his death. Later he is seen defending one Harley Barnes, a clergyman charged with Red associations. Quentin clearly has no use for the Committee. They seem to him ruthless hypocrites, "hateful men." Yet he has also only limited admiration for his client. He doubts that were positions reversed, Barnes would be much more tolerant than his inquisitors. And in the clergyman's monotonous denials, Quentin detects a discouragingly negative outlook. What is it that Barnes really favors? If Quentin in these sections speaks at all for Miller, then there is some sympathy for former leftists at bay, but no clear endorsement of any current political alignment.

RELIGIOUS ASPECTS. Toward the end of the play Quentin comes to realize poignantly that he and other human beings meet "unblessed," not in a pretty make-believe world of artificial fruits and trees, "that lie of Eden," but "after the Fall, after many, many deaths." The "Fall" in the play's title thus refers in some way to "The Fall of Man," and recalls the Biblical account of the sin of Adam and Eve and of their expulsion by God from their earthly paradise, the garden of Eden. Actually, Miller is not mainly concerned with the religious doctrines derived from this part of the Book of Genesis. He is not, for instance, like the great English poet, John Milton, who makes use of the narrative in his *Paradise Lost* to "justify the ways of God to man."

Miller seems rather to seize upon the traditional concept of the Fall as a vivid, telling way of expressing what Quentin has discovered about himself and about his fellow men. If the word "Eden" suggests innocence and untainted goodness, then, whatever the cause, this world today is no Eden. And anyone who would picture himself or those he admires as ideal figures in some such idyllic environment is deceiving himself and certain to encounter eventually some measure of bitter disillusionment.

Again, if the Fall throughout the ages signified that men were not altogether irreproachable, but were subject at least to evil inclinations, then this, too, is what Quentin observes. He, who with reason has always thought of himself as a decent, civilized man, has recognized that he can be profoundly selfish and can hate with terrible fury. He has also noted how his mother, Elsie, Mickey, and Maggie have on occasion showed treacherous impulses.

And even the admirable Holga has hinted at darker moments in her own complex life as a German during the Nazi regime. Miller does not use such an awareness to suggest the need for some form of spiritual redemption based upon new, more rewarding relationships between man and his God. His Quentin does not think in terms of sin and atonement, or prayer for divine help and guidance. Rebecca, in *The Crucible*, can say en route to execution, "Let you fear nothing! Another judgment waits us all!" But Quentin sees himself as pleading before an empty bench. In his secular universe, only Quentin can pass judgment on Quentin.

Yet God is mentioned. God to Quentin is "what happened," or "what is." God is whatever bitter truth the human being must face squarely or perish. God also represents the concept of unlimited capacity to love. Thus when human beings foolishly claim that they can love others infinitely, they are guilty of a great and dangerous lie. To Quentin, then, one comes to terms with God, that is the truth about life or "what is," by acknowledging one's past responsibility for harm to others and one's ever-present potential for future harmful action. None of us, in other words, can ever say with certainty that under no circumstance would we help build a concentration camp. Yet there is some hope in the very facing of such a humbling, distasteful idea. For when we sell ourselves the "lie of Eden" and make foolish pretenses to innocence and limitless love, we follow a course of guilty evasion that can culminate in cruel, hypocritical betrayals or suicidal despair.

MORAL ASPECTS. In *All My Sons,* Miller gives us a man who is defensively obtuse about the true nature of human responsibility. In boldly rationalizing his shipping of the defective airplane parts, Ed Keller is trying to excuse the inexcusable. In *Death of a Salesman,* Willy finds it impossible to understand how Biff can claim, "We never told the truth for ten minutes in this house!" Willy constantly lies about himself and gives his sons a false picture of the life they must face. In *The Crucible,* telling the truth is also the major issue. Rebecca, Elizabeth and John find that they cannot compromise with reality, as Hale suggests, and heroically endure great suffering. Here, in *After the Fall,* Maggie dies because she wilfully refuses to face her moral responsibility. Quentin and Holga come to terms with truth and retain some hope. So in this play, as in the earlier ones, acknowledging responsibility and bravely accepting the consequences would seem to be Miller's major moral concern.

Cruelty and betrayal, however, are also given attention. There is noteworthy emphasis upon the bitter denunciation of Quentin's father by his mother at a time when a business failure left him sorely vulnerable. And Quentin sees himself betrayed when his mother uses him to point up his father's shortcomings. There are also contemptuous attacks by Elsie, Louise, and Maggie, that inflict painful wounds. And Quentin is uncertain to what extent his own subtler failures helped to bring about the untimely deaths of Lou and Maggie.

PSYCHOLOGICAL ASPECTS. Quentin traces much of his later anxiety and confusion to the images of himself created by his mother during his boyhood. On the one hand she flattered him with lofty predictions of guaranteed greatness. He thus developed a certain smugness and was perhaps too ready to accept the adulation of a naive Felice or the emotional hero-worship of an immature Maggie. He was also accustomed to constant attention and praise, as Louise pettishly remarks. At the same time, the very ferocity with which his mother tore down his father's self-respect had unfortunate effects upon the boy. For one thing, it ruined his respect for the older man, thus, in effect, depriving him of one parent. Second, it somehow left him shaken and insecure, perhaps not wholly certain that he is any more worthy of notice than his father was. Quentin speaks of himself as always trying to prove something. He does seek commendation. And he is particularly sensitive when Elsie, Louise, and Maggie use the same bitter tone his mother once employed. It may also be mentioned that the troubled Maggie is the product of an irregular love union. Her father refuses to acknowledge her. Her mother, who engaged in illicit affairs but could act with excessive prudery, is clearly a terror symbol. She once tried to kill the girl to keep her pure, and Maggie is still haunted by the awful memory.

IMAGES AND SYMBOLS. Miller often uses key objects or images to make his dramatic points more clearly. Larry's tree and the letter are used effectively in *All My Sons,* and Willy's cars and Biff's stolen football and basketballs are important in *Death of a Salesman.* In *The Crucible,* much is made of the poppet, the chains, and John's signed confession.

In *After the Fall,* the ruined tower of the concentration camp, always visible in the open set, represents all the barbarous cruelty man can inflict at his worst. Holga's flowers, by contrast, suggest all that is fresh and hopeful. Louise is usually seen with an apron on, because she is to be seen mainly as housewife. And Quentin's masterly brief is used to show how he is admired by Lou and Elsie but cannot impress Louise who has no interest in this type of work. Felice's removing of bandages from her nose brings out Quentin's casual, half-amused participation in the minor concerns of a pretty client. The toy sailboat brought from Atlantic City is a bribe used to regain the trust of a small boy who feels cheated. And Maggie's white wedding dress suggests the innocence that both she and Quentin mistakenly think can be retained, despite sordid past experiences.

As for images, mention has already been made of the contrast drawn between an illusory Eden, complete with fake foliage, and the unblessed world as it really exists. The play's most striking metaphor, however, is that of the "idiot child." Holga tells Quentin that she, too, has memories she would like to erase. But after much anguish, she has come to realize that our lives are what we make of them, and we cannot alter the past by wishing it had been different. Neither can we avoid its returning constantly to demand our recognition. Her solution is to treat it with the determined affection a mother might give an idiot child. The mother wishes the child were more attractive, but acknowledging it as hers, she gives it at least as much love as she can. Tormented by his own too vivid recollections, Quentin finds this a hard saying. At the end, however, he, too, hopes that he can with courage love and forgive what has so distressed him in his own life, the urge to let others die that he might live.

FORM AND STYLE. In *Death of a Salesman*, Miller has Willy in moments of crisis slip back to relive, half-consciously, crucial past scenes. For the most part, Willy is distracted. Hence, while these relived memories now become part of his present experience, he is not sufficiently aware of the lapses to evaluate what he recalls. In the earlier play, too, there are some scenes *outside* of Willy's consciousness, such as that in which Linda tells their sons about his recent business setbacks. Because of this element, the set has at least some semblance of a real house with real rooms. Biff and Happy are actually occupying a bedroom, and are not merely two more of Willy's memories.

After the Fall, going further, takes place entirely in Quentin's mind. The basic form of the play is that of the dramatic monologue. Quentin has dropped in to talk things over with an unseen "Listener." Sometimes there is the barest indication of some reaction upon the part of this vaguely established being. But throughout, Quentin does the talking; and the memory scenes are played against a bare, cavernous set, done in neutral shades, with functional blocks and ledges used to represent a variety of places. Characters drift in and out, as Quentin happens to think of them, with one remembered incident sometimes "calling to mind," as if simultaneously, a rapid flashing recollection of other people, who then also appear for an instant.

Three differences are apparent when this format is compared with that of *Death of a Salesman*. First of all, there is more extensive use of this overlapping technique. Willy Loman sometimes seems to talk simultaneously to the present Charlie and the long-vanished Ben. And he hears the laugh of his Boston mistress, while talking to Linda during one of his memory scenes. But never is there the constant effect of ebb and flow as when Quentin's remembered figures drift in and out of his thoughts.

The second variation is that, in *After the Fall*, we never get more than one basic point of view. We see only scenes in which Quentin personally has taken part. We see only the aspects of other people's personalities that were revealed to him or that he remembers. We never hear the private opinions of anyone else or get the chance to encounter them in a relationship that does not include the hero. In a work that has so little of the orderly time sequence of a play like *The Crucible,* the continued presence of Quentin is a unifying factor. In addition, there is some psychological interest in observing just what one particular mind would see as crucial in forty years of varied life experiences, or what the impact of other individuals would be on such an individual. At the same time, there is none of the balance secured when others talk frankly out of earshot of the character concerned. And in many instances the other characters can never be adequately developed. They are memory wraiths rather than people. Finally, it makes it imperative that Quentin, as central, all-important figure, be interesting enough as a personality to sustain interest and carry much of the play. Not all critics agreed that Quentin was so fascinating a character.

The third distinction is that Quentin has much more self-awareness than Willy. As he relives past experiences, Quentin evaluates and judges. Everything that he recalls is treated as evidence by this thoughtful lawyer, and weighed for what it contributes to his developing over-all view of life. For instance, when he recalls some of Louise's criticisms, he is inclined to accept as valid some accusations that he denied at the time. In conventional plays the "flashback," or scene from the past, was used mainly to provide exposition, or information necessary so that audiences might understand present happenings. In *Death of a Salesman,* Miller used his memory scenes artistically, not only for exposition but as part of the drama's main action. Willy's vivid memories help drive him to his final suicidal crash. *After the Fall* goes one step further. The remembered incidents are not only exposition and an integral factor in Quentin's climactic decision to greet Holga. They are also weighed carefully by a reflective, extremely self-conscious individual. And it is in Quentin's careful consideration of what past events may be seen to signify, that Arthur Miller voices his most painstakingly hammered-out theories and conclusions.

REVIEW QUESTIONS AND ANSWERS

1. In one passage Quentin speaks of himself as having been "injured" by the women in his life. Is there basis for this charge?

ANSWER: It would appear that Quentin's mother did cause him to be somewhat vulnerable later in life. By her predictions of greatness, she may have induced him to set for himself impossible standards. By her flattering praise, she may have given him too high an opinion of his own virtue. By her denunciation of his father, she may in the long run have lessened his confidence in himself as a man. And by her failure to play fair with him, as in the Atlantic City incident, she may have helped create in him a deep-rooted uncertainty as to the advisability of loving and trusting. On the other hand, his mother did plead for him when his father insisted that he go into the family business, thus freeing him to get the training necessary for his later career.

Louise, too, played a part in shaking his self-esteem. Her accusations that he ignores her and seeks only everybody's adulation obviously disturb him. One minute he thinks he is a good, faithful, and relatively successful husband and father. The next he is rejected as withdrawn, cold, and unfeeling. Yet even if Louise's castigation is eventually shattering, he does have with her a good home for some seven years, and there is much evidence that his career developed well during this period. Lou, for instance, finds his brief superior.

Maggie, of course, causes him great distress. And her tragic death makes him feel guilty. Yet it is through his experiences with her that he eventually works his way through to the solacing truth that enables him to seek a future with Holga. So, while the women did cause him worry and anxiety, they also contributed toward his ultimate progress.

2. How does Quentin compare as a personality with the heroes of other Miller dramas?

ANSWER: Like both Ed Keller and Willy Loman, Quentin starts with a relatively high opinion of himself, although deep within him there are suppressed misgivings. Keller thinks he is a good citizen and family man. Willy believes that he has given his boys good advice. Quentin sees himself as a strong, gentle, civilized person motivated by generous, unselfish considerations. Keller comes to understand that he did a terrible thing to his other "sons" in shipping the defective parts. Willy never does clearly comprehend where he went wrong, any more than does Maggie in *After the Fall*. Quentin, however, does become aware of his dangerously selfish inclinations. And he alone of the three survives to put his new knowledge into practice.

Unlike Keller and Willy, Quentin works out his recognition very much by himself. The other two both have disillusioned sons who angrily try to make their respective fathers face the bitter facts. At the same time, the others also have extremely loyal and helpful wives who try to protect them at all times. Quentin's wives tend to be as accusing as the other men's sons. Yet eventually, he works out a solution by thinking over what they and his other relatives and friends have told him.

Finally, Quentin the intellectual is up against a more subtle form of testing. Keller, Willy, and John Proctor, in *The Crucible,* are so involved that death is the only possible answer. Quentin is ostensibly only deciding whether or not to meet a girl at an airport. Yet alone, having given up his career, Quentin, too, is close to a despair that is a kind of death, or possibly its forerunner. But in achieving some sort of workable solution, Quentin will go on to live.

3. Why do Quentin's memories rouse guilt feelings in him, and how does he resolve his psychological problems?

ANSWER: Quentin's distress is caused largely by the fact that he seems, often against his will, to have hurt those to whom he was closely allied. He meant to be a good husband to Louise, but she found him cold and selfish. He intended to show Maggie only devoted concern, but she bitterly denounced him as a liar and a hypocrite. He wanted only to show his loyalty to the accused Lou, but the latter, in despair apparently, committed suicide.

As a civilized man, Quentin finds it hard to understand how he could have failed so miserably. And what is even more disturbing, he cannot see how he could have avoided certain unfortunate situations. He could certainly be technically faithful to Louise, but could he always have known how to please her? And could he have wholly suppressed brief, flickering interest in others? He could take care of Maggie's business demands and look after her when she was sick. But could he help some feeling of revulsion when he thought of her past affairs?

As he thinks about such matters, Quentin comes to recognize, although with repugnance, certain profoundly selfish instincts that are his despite all his pretensions to idealism. He knows too that they are neither wholly predictable nor easily controlled. Yet once having faced the grim fact that he has given before, and may again give, disheartening evidence of baser tendencies, he will try bravely to accept his human limitations and once more risk some commitment. With Holga, who also has learned not to expect the impossible, he may yet work out a fairly satisfactory life.

INCIDENT AT VICHY

(1964)

CHARACTERS

LEBEAU. A shaggy, bearded young artist, weak from lack of food, who keeps on talking loudly to stifle his panic.

BAYARD. A blunt, vigorous, capable young electrician, who believes in Socialism but is prepared to use ingenuity and skill to escape from its Nazi representatives.

MARCHAND. A pompous, assertive businessman, certain that he is indispensable, and irked that his arrest forces him to miss an office appointment.

MONCEAU. A somewhat haughty, fastidious actor who insists that survival may hinge upon one's convincing air of confidence.

GYPSY. A furtive, wary little man staunchly maintaining that he has not stolen the heavy pot he so jealously guards.

WAITER. An affable, willing employee of the cafe next door, who cannot see how such genial German patrons could possibly seek his death.

BOY. A worried, bewildered fourteen-year-old, who begs only that some friend return to his destitute mother the wedding ring he was sent out to pawn before being detained.

MAJOR. A pale, wounded German line officer, who, if not opposed to the Nazi drive against Jews, is revolted by the barbarous methods used to carry it out.

OLD JEW. A poor, frail, bearded man, in his seventies, who quietly murmurs prayers and clutches a pathetic sackcloth bundle.

LEDUC. An astute psychiatrist and French combat officer, who, when not trying to organize an escape attempt, concentrates on getting the rest to face up to some hard truths.

VON BERG. A humane, cultivated Austrian prince, no longer young, who maintains that man's only hope against such evil forces as those of the vulgar, savage Nazis lies in the courageous acts of heroic individuals.

PROFESSOR HOFFMAN. A cold, relentless scientist, with no sympathy either for his Jewish victims or the squeamish German major.

FERRAND. The cafe proprietor, understandably in awe of his Nazi customers, who yet risks passing on some explosive information to his unfortunate waiter.

OTHER CHARACTERS. The interrogation program is conducted with the aid of a' police captain, two detectives, and a guard. In addition, as the play comes to an end, four new prisoners are brought in for questioning.

SETTING

Played through without intermission, the drama is set in the town of Vichy, France, in 1942. The place is a large, bare, rather grimy room in which prisoners sit on a long bench while awaiting the questioning that goes on in an adjacent room. Stark and dreary, it has a disheartening effect on those under arrest.

PLOT ANALYSIS

On a morning in 1942, six men and a boy wait uneasily in a detention room in Vichy, France. By now France is out of World War II, having surrendered to the Nazi Germans. But the country's southern part, around Vichy, is in theory "unoccupied" by the conquerors. Nevertheless, Germans were in the car when these prisoners were taken. So they wonder with alarm what is back of their arrest.

The first to pose disturbing questions to the rest is Lebeau, a bearded, rumpled artist, faint from lack of food. The only one to reassure him is Marchand, a self-important businessman edgy lest he miss an important appointment. He asserts that this is merely a routine checking of identification papers, since Vichy now is so crowded with foreigners. Lebeau, however, suspects that all here are Jewish, and that the arrest has something to do with the Nazi campaign against Jews. He recalls sadly that his family could have left for America three years ago, but his mother would not give up her brass bed and other treasured household articles. Lebeau is particularly irked because a man in the arresting party measured his nose before having him seized. Bayard, a sturdy, forceful electrician, tells him that he must blame everything upon the power-hungry monopolies. Bayard is a Socialist.

For a moment Marchand and a middle-aged waiter join in disapproving comments upon a less reputable fellow-prisoner, a gypsy, clutching a pot they are sure he must have stolen. Lebeau, however, criticizes them for idolizing those whose sole virtue is working hard. Have not the industrious Germans now overrun Europe? At this point, a worn-looking, wounded young German major enters. The waiter greets him as an old customer, but the major is politely aloof.

Thereupon two detectives and a police captain bring in three new prisoners. With the group is the professor, an authoritative civilian, who sends the police out to round up more. The businessman, Marchand, impatiently follows the professor in for questioning. Meanwhile, one of the new arrivals, Leduc, an erstwhile French officer, recognizes the major as a member of an outfit he fought against in the battle of Amiens.

The major leaves, and Leduc questions his fellow captives. He is perturbed when Lebeau relates again that his nose was measured. He is even more alarmed when Bayard, the electrician, tells of a train in the Vichy freight yards, with a Polish engineer. The freight cars were jammed with imprisoned men, women and even babies, under intolerable conditions. Bayard notes, too, that gypsies, like Jews, are condemned by the Nazis as inferior people. So the others try to get the gypsy to admit having stolen the pot. For if he was arrested as a thief, this may not be a Nazi purge.

Bayard, however, convinced that they are headed for concentration camps, urges all to look around for some useful tool to unhinge a freight-car door. He takes the handle from the gypsy's pot, when the latter is called in. Disputing his pessimistic view is Monceau, a carefully dressed, lordly young actor, who cannot believe that Germans, always such an admirable audience, could kill off great numbers of Jews.

Entering the debate now is Von Berg, a kindly, aging Austrian prince. He is pleased to learn that Leduc, by profession a psychiatrist, studied in Vienna at the medical school, with which his cousin, Baron Kessler, is connected. Leduc is noncommital about the baron, but all are relieved that the prince, a Catholic, has also been arrested. For, again this suggests that the rest were not seized for being Jewish. Von Berg surprises Leduc by his obvious contempt for the Nazis. Leduc had thought all aristocrats reactionary. Von Berg finds Nazis unspeakably vulgar and can see how such brutes would be cruel and savage. Yet he is forced by Monceau to admit that not all the artistically sensitive always refrain from inhuman acts. All, however, are suddenly cheered by the reappearance of Marchand with a pass to freedom. They feel certain that he is Jewish. So if he has been freed, there is hope. All look over their own papers, trusting that they are in order.

The old Jew shows signs of collapse, and Leduc takes his pulse. Ferrand, the cafe proprietor, brings in coffee for the Germans, and Bayard is summoned. Monceau, the actor, warns him to look confident. Bayard replies that his Socialist faith will sustain him. Some day the working class will triumph. Von Berg asks,

are not most Nazis from that class? The prince admits that any
faith today is laudable, but thinks that man's one hope lies with
the few in all classes who have integrity. He remembers how the
humble folk who worked for him all but worshipped Hitler.
Ferrand then comes out and whispers to his captive waiter the
terrifying information that the prisoners are destined to be burned
in Polish furnaces. He adds that the Nazis within are examining all
suspects to ascertain whether or not they have been circumcised.
Bayard leaves with dignity, as music is heard from the cafe.

Leduc tries to organize an escape attempt, but Von Berg is too
weak physically, and Monceau is unwilling. He finds the furnace
story incredible. Von Berg, however, believes it. The Nazis slaughter
Jews to prove their own warped sincerity. The waiter is called, and
there are sounds of blows. Coming out, the major and the professor argue, for the former is sickened by the procedures. After
all, he himself is circumcised. Over the professor's protests, he
leaves for a brief walk.

The young boy offers to help Leduc in his escape move. But
Monceau holds out, and Lebeau, the artist, is faint from hunger.
Monceau tells of leaving Paris. He was playing Cyrano, a great,
desirable role, but finally fled. He still, however, discounts the
atrocity reports. Von Berg replies that the Nazi came and took
his castle musician and killed him. The boy begs him to return
for him a wedding ring he was sent to pawn for his impoverished
mother. Leduc tries vainly to bait Monceau into joining him.
Lebeau remarks that with so much hostility, it is hard not to feel
vaguely guilty. Monceau argues that if he obeys laws, he will go free.
After all, these are French police. The boy gives his ring to the sympathetic Von Berg and starts to run. But the returning major warns
all that escape is impossible. Although he dislikes the business, the
major will not let them go. He has no use for their love and respect.

As he shouts, the professor re-enters. The major shoots off his
revolver and suggests to the idealistic Leduc that were he freed
he would go off and leave the others. Leduc is unsure. Lebeau is
called and leaves tiredly. Monceau follows, with a brave smile,
and after him goes the boy. Leduc begs Von Berg to go afterwards
and inform his wife. The doctor is irritable knowing that the Austrian will survive. Von Berg confesses he was once close to
suicide, and says he will help the doctor's family. Leduc finds
it ironic that he was taken while going after toothache medicine
for a wife he no longer loves. When they come for the old
Jew, his bundle opens. It is merely feathers. Leduc says man
should accept his nature—he is not reasonable but full of murder.
Von Berg counters that there are still idealists. Leduc then says
that all men have some hatred for others—for Jews or for any
whose sufferings they have thankfully escaped. Did not Von Berg

himself tolerate his cousin, Baron Kessler, even though the other persecuted Jews? Leduc wants Von Berg to acknowledge some responsibility even for the Nazi crimes he condemns.

Von Berg, disturbed by this accusation, is called. Within moments he returns and gives his own pass to freedom to Leduc. The latter now feels guilty, but takes it and leaves, agreeing to return the boy's ring. After a pause, the professor enters and discovers the escape. As he summons the guard, the major stares, half angrily, half sadly, at the tired but resolute Von Berg. As the play ends, four new prisoners are herded in.

ANALYSES OF THE MAJOR CHARACTERS

THE PRINCE: This aging, physically frail Austrian nobleman is by nature a gentle, courteous individual, modest and unassuming. A man accustomed to wealth and the refinements of living, he has a gracious manner that suggests a kindly, reasonably generous personality. He tried to shelter and protect the musicians he admired. He now considers bribing officials to let the psychiatrist go, or at least supplying funds to the latter's wife and children.

Yet for all his benign, self-deprecating, unassertive air, he gives evidence of possessing a keen, alert mind. He has strong views on questions relating to the Nazis and ably defends them, pointing out the fallacies in the arguments of others. He is quick, for instance, to dispute the electrician's assumption that the Nazi movement is not backed by the common people. At the same time, he is capable of appreciating flaws in his own reasoning, when such are pointed out to him. He realizes, for example, that he has perhaps been too ready to assume that all Nazis are hostile to great art.

A retiring type, he is not anxious to become involved in situations that might prove embarrassing. He does not really want to have to return the boy's ring to the unfortunate mother or to inform the psychiatrist's wife that her husband will never return. He admits that he has never, in fact, felt wholly at ease with women. Moreover, when he finally recognized the evils of Nazism, his instincts were to flee rather than fight. And he found the thought of suicide seductive. Yet he does have courage. He does agree to undertake the difficult interviews with the boy's mother and the doctor's wife. He does finally offer, despite his lack of physical strength, to take part in the escape attempt. He does brush aside with haughty authority the restraining arm of the insolent Nazi. And above all, having accepted half-unwillingly the doctor's charge that he has failed to battle sufficiently against the Nazi evils he hates, he gives up his own precious pass to freedom. Like John Proctor in *The Crucible*, once this basically good man finds his proper course of action, he pursues it even though he is obviously rather astonished to find himself playing the hero's role.

LEDUC: A wiry, restless, intense man, Leduc is both doctor and
military officer, intellectual and man of action. From the first he
is someone who will not readily accept an unpleasant situation. As
he is brought in, there is indication that he vehemently resisted
the arrest. And he is soon challenging the major to justify such
treatment of a French combat officer. He is also prepared to organize
a daring break, and uses all his skills to shame the actor into par-
ticipating in the attempt. He also later makes a quite eloquent plea
to the apparently wavering major to get him to let the suspects go.

Like the prince, he too has given much thought to the phenomenon
of Nazism, and has some firm opinions. Yet he also is receptive to
new approaches. Never having known well a man expressing so
cogently the aristocratic view, he listens attentively and respectfully
to what the prince contributes. At the same time, while conceding
that the nobleman has made valid points, he relentlessly drives
home the idea that by not actively taking up cudgels against Nazism
the prince has shirked responsibility. And then, having succeeded
only too well, he is obviously appalled at what responsibility he
must now shoulder, having accepted the prince's pass.

For all his high-minded idealism, the doctor is a moody man. Angered, he can be rude and insulting, but is often ready to apologize
soon afterward. He was captured because he came into town seeking
codeine to ease his wife's toothache. He is furious with himself
for having run such a risk for a woman he no longer deeply loves.
Hence, for a moment, vindictively, he urges the prince to paint the
facts at their grimmest and thus make her suffer, too. Yet almost
in the next breath, he regrets his outburst and stops insisting that
all her hopes be destroyed. Even when most fervently preaching
altruism, he is honest regarding his own limitations. When the
major asks if he would accept his own liberation, knowing that the
rest were to die, he hesitates. And the major laughs, cruelly and
triumphantly. And, in actual fact, he does in the end go off with
the prince's pass. Yet he goes agreeing to deliver the boy's ring,
and there is every indication that if he survives he will probably
accept his share of responsibility that he has so clearly recognized.

BAYARD: The sturdy, capable electrician again interestingly com-
bines the practical and the speculative. He is not one to avoid facing
ugly facts. He has heard about the trainloads of captives headed
for Poland, and he has few illusions about the reception awaiting
them there. Yet he is determined to take whatever opportunities
present themselves for survival. He tells the others about the possibility of removing freight-car door hinges, and prudently equips
himself with the handle of the gypsy's pot to use as a makeshift tool.
He is a fairly controlled, level-headed man even in this dire peril,
and would seem to have a fair chance, if any of them have, to work
out some means of escape.

At the same time, he is a convinced Socialist, with an almost mystical faith in a future that will see the oppressors humbled and poor men enjoying the good life in an atmosphere of peace and brotherhood. The prince makes it clear that not all the upper-class people are Nazi supporters, and that many members of the servant group idolize Hitler. But Bayard still derives some hope from being part of a great historic movement that would eventually lead to freedom for the masses. And so he can walk in with dignity to face his persecutors.

LE BEAU: Faint from hunger but inclined to be boisterous, the artist is a badly frightened man. Sometimes, in fact, he talks almost foolishly because the silence is even more terrifying. He is deeply conscious of the way his dignity as a man has been affronted. His nose has been measured as if he were some type of odd specimen, and he has even been denied the right to order a cup of coffee.

Although he suggests that an overemphasis upon work may have helped to build up the Nazi menace, he actually is hard put to see any sense whatsoever in what is happening in the world. For his part, he is in Vichy because his stubborn mother refused to leave a few treasured household goods and head for free America. And he was captured because he impulsively went out for a pre-breakfast walk. Interpreting such events is as ridiculous as attributing exact literal meanings to his paintings. Weakening further physically as the morning wears on, he seems almost dazed when finally called.

MARCHAND: This elegant, somewhat supercilious actor has always placed great reliance upon presenting a good appearance. Carefully groomed, he is prepared to approach his captors with an air of assurance. It is his contention that they will then be much less apt to treat him with the surly contempt they reserve for those who cringe.

Actually, he has known before this what it means to be afraid. In Paris he was playing Cyrano, a role he had long coveted. Yet fearful that some books disapproved by the Germans be traced to him, he had fled to Vichy. He is also, in truth, badly frightened now. Yet he keeps assuring himself and others that the Germans who so heartily applauded his performances could not possibly want his life. And with the almost pathetic hope that he can charm the present very critical audience of interrogators, he will not allow himself to be cajoled or taunted by the doctor into joining any escape attempt. He is a fairly selfish individual. There is no evidence that he gives much thought to the plight of the others. But as he musters all his dignity for a last brave audition, there is something admirable about him.

COMMENTARY ON *INCIDENT AT VICHY*

FAVORABLE RECEPTION. Presented only a few months after Arthur Miller's much discussed *After the Fall,* this shorter play about Nazi crimes during World War II opened in December, 1964. Unlike some earlier Miller dramas, it was not obviously controversial. It involved no seemingly intimate revelations such as those in *After the Fall.* And it played before audiences generally disposed to condemn the Nazi outrages it decries. On the whole, critical response was favorable. Some reviews, it is true, found little novelty in the ideas and thought the characters rather arbitrarily chosen to represent specific points of view, rather than to stand as interesting individuals. But many found the work a deeply moving experience.

SUSPENSEFUL TREATMENT. For a play that deals so much with ideas, *Incident at Vichy* is still, first and foremost, a lively, exciting theatre piece. The initial situation is provocative enough. Ten strangers are herded into a barren waiting room of some sort. Why are they being held? And who are they as people? Then as the horrible truth is revealed, various possibilities of escape are suggested. If the merchant is given a pass, others may likewise be freed. Since the Catholic Austrian has been arrested, it may not be an anti-Jewish move at all. Again, perhaps the major, evidently hostile to the investigations, will give the captives a chance. And all the time the threat of a terrible doom hangs over the gradually diminishing group. And toward the end there is the powerful confrontation scene between doctor and prince, culminating in the latter's heroic sacrifice and the former's escape. Dramatically, this is an effective presentation.

UNUSUAL TECHNIQUES. Ever since the days of the ancient Greeks, there has been interest in the so-called "unities." A play's structure is supposedly tightened if the action occurs within about twenty-four hours (unity of time) and within a relatively small area (unity of place). *Incident at Vichy* has only one set, the large, unprepossessing waiting room, and is performed without any intermission break. The slightly less than two hours of playing time corresponds to the time that such an investigation might believably take. So the unity of time is more precise than it is ordinarily.

Only certain of the characters are given names at all. And these seem to have symbolic implications. The prince is Von Berg; *Berg* is the German word for mountain, and the prince represents an aristocratic or upper-class view. The business man is Marchand, from the French word for merchant; and the artist is LeBeau, suggesting the beautiful that art attempts to create. Some others are merely a waiter, a boy, an old Jew, and the major. There are, of course, references to the home lives of a few. Mention is made of the psychiatrist's wife, and the mothers of the artist and the boy. There are also allusions to the domestic arrangements of the prince's castle. But, to some extent, these are clearly "typical" figures, representing the various categories of people caught up in the Nazi holocaust.

THE EVILS OF NAZISM. As regards the World War II horrors, the playwright seems to have three objectives. First of all, he clearly wants them to be remembered lest similar outrages recur. With this in view, he vividly suggests the sufferings undergone. He tells of locked freight cars jammed with doomed men, women, and children. And in the scenes actually presented, he shows the coldness and cruelty of the persecutors and the fear and anguish of those trapped. He suggests the terrible waste of it all as artist, doctor, workman, and prince are herded to destruction along with an aged, pious man and an inoffensive young boy. In addition, he points up the terrible insults to human dignity. The guards will not even answer civil questions, and handle prisoners with coarse brutality. A request to be allowed to order coffee is denied, and medical examinations for circumcision are conducted in such a gross manner as to humiliate and embarrass the suspect. Everything, in short, in the play is calculated to make decent individuals recognize the awful degradation and misery to which rather ordinary, far from criminal human beings were subjected a generation ago simply because they were Jewish.

Secondly, Miller appears to pose questions regarding the course adopted by the Nazis. The artist, who professes actually to find little meaning in the whole horror story, does ruefully suggest some imbalance created by overstressing work. The electrician sees it as a painful but necessary historical stage preceding the era of peace and brotherhood. The prince sees the persecutions as a perverse proof of Nazi consistency or sincerity. They not only aver hatred—they put it shamelessly into practice. In another sense, however, since they are essentially negative with little to their credit, they are trying to prove that they exist and can do something to stagger the imagination. The psychiatrist, in turn, sees the persecuting Nazis as mere extensions of the average man. All men, he says, have their "Jews," or someone they despise. The Nazis merely are better organized and carry their prejudices further.

Finally, Miller seems to be pointing possible explanations as to why ordinary, well-meaning people defend themselves ineffectually against such a menace. First of all, of course, some are physically weak. Here the old Jew, the boy, and the prince are not able to fight, and the artist is faint from hunger.

In addition, some are simply imprudent. The artist's mother should have left the possessions in view of the threat to the lives of all.

The artist knows that he should not have risked the walk. The doctor wonders if he should have jeopardized his life by going out to seek a remedy for his wife's pain, that would soon have passed.

Then, too, there is a sort of blind incredulity that such horrors can really occur. The actor cannot believe that enthusiastic German audiences could execute harmless people. The waiter thinks of the Germans as pleasant cafe patrons. Most hesitate to believe that the rumors can be true about the gas chambers in concentration camps. There is talk of the law that is sure to protect the law-abiding; and even the normally perceptive prince is apparently loath to believe that his esteemed cousin, the baron, could be connected with anything so hateful.

Above all, however, there is that selfishness that keeps even good men from banding effectively together. The businessman has no interest in the fate of the rest. The actor has no wish to join in the escape conspiracy. The businessman and the waiter join in voicing contempt for their fellow-prisoner, the gypsy. And no one is eager to return the ring to the boy's mother. The psychiatrist talks of mutual responsibility. But even he is silent when the major sneeringly asks if he would accept the chance to live even if the others were to die. All in all, when men are afraid, the play suggests, they do not always realize that in unity lies their strength.

LINKS WITH OTHER MILLER WORKS. *Incident at Vichy* is connected most obviously with the immediately preceding play, *After the Fall*. In that work the ruined tower of the concentration camp looms up ever-present in Quentin's mind. And Holga's idea that no one is wholly innocent who survived such persecutions, seems to anticipate the psychiatrist's talk of responsibility to the prince.

There are other echoes, too. The question of responsibility had been raised in *All My Sons*. Ed Keller, according to his son, had no right to ship defective plane parts merely to make money for his own family. He had obligations to the group as a whole. *Death of a Salesman* explores, among other things, the capacity of anxious men to delude themselves. Biff and Willy both talk as though the sporting goods manufacturer, Oliver, were going to lend thousands to a former employee with no security to offer. Here, because the prisoners want to believe that they will not be killed, they almost succeed at times in convincing themselves that the investigation is merely "routine."

Like *The Crucible*, this play also deals with people caught up in a monstrous attack upon the rights of the individual. In both, as also in connection with the Congressional probes in *After the Fall*, there is much soul-searching, as those accused try to face facts and

make decisions. The artist's admission that the accusations themselves create in him vague feelings of guilt recalls the troubled
remarks of Lou and Mickey in *After the Fall*. And the prince's
half-angry, almost reluctant heroism calls to mind John Proctor
in *The Crucible,* who also had no great relish for a martyr's role,
but finally made at great cost a noble decision.

REVIEW QUESTIONS AND ANSWERS

1. Why does Leduc tell the worried prince that he wants his responsibility, not his guilt?

ANSWER: Were the psychiatrist trying merely to make the prince
feel unhappy, he would not be doing anything very admirable. It
must be remembered, however, that at this point the situation is
such that Leduc assumes that he will die and the prince live. Inasmuch as the prince is not Jewish, there is an excellent chance
that he will be given a pass to freedom.

If, under such circumstances, the prince feels merely a depressing
sense of guilt, he may be drawn more strongly than ever to the
idea of suicide. But if he accepts the burden or "responsibility,"
he may go on to oppose the Nazi atrocities in some effective fashion and thus help to avoid future outrages such as the one he
has witnessed in this Vichy incident.

Actually, the psychiatrist succeeds only too well. The prince, who
has already declared that he believes that the future of civilization
rests with the heroic individual, does accept responsibility. He is
old and weak, without any immediate family depending on him.
The doctor is younger and more vigorous, and has a wife and
children. He is clearly an idealist and a man with skills valuable
to many. Hence, the prince, who had perhaps not been firm enough
in opposing the pro-Nazi policies of his admired relative, Baron
Kessler, makes up for any past hesitancy by giving his pass to
Leduc. It is then up to the doctor, in turn, to take up the challenge
and go on struggling against injustice.

2. Explain the use of the word "incident" in the title, indicating
how the play's format has been chosen to emphasize the ironic
point made by using this word.

ANSWER: An incident is often a "minor event," something perhaps
not very important in itself but linked with matters of greater
significance. During the World War II era, thousands, even mil-
lions, of unfortunate people died as the result of the Nazi program
to destroy the Jewish people. When such great numbers are involved, ten, or rather eight, lives are extremely few. Their hearings
are handled with dispatch and their fates are sealed in a matter

of minutes. From the point of view of their captors, they are minor "routine" cases, not worth wasting much time over. A few perfunctory queries, the cursory examinations of documents; and they will be doomed to horrible deaths. There is no defense counsel, no jury, no chance even to take care of small personal obligations. And the swift dramatic movement and the absence of any intermission emphasize the indecent swiftness with which these men's fates are decided.

Miller, however, uses the term "incident" ironically. In his view, what happens to these ten men, or to any human beings, is important. He therefore reveals their hopes, their dreams, their fears and sufferings, in order to make us care, even if their captors do not, what happens to them. If the individual has any rights, the young boy, the actor, the waiter, the old Jew, and the gypsy have them, just as much as do the doctor and the prince. And any "incident," that tramples down their human dignity, is, according to the playwright, a crime to be angrily denounced.

3. Why do the prisoners find it so hard to accept the warning of the electrician and the cafe owner that they are destined to be killed?

ANSWER: Humanly speaking, of course, they do not want to face so horrible a prospect. They may not be totally unaccustomed to being afraid. The actor was alarmed enough to flee from Paris, even if it meant giving up his coveted Cyrano role. The artist knew that to take a walk was dangerous, and the boy apparently only scurried forth because he had to pawn his mother's ring. But even having lived under tension, they still think of themselves as ordinary decent people, not hunted criminals. And the idea that those they do not know and have never harmed would want to send them off to a flaming death, is not only too awful to contemplate, but almost preposterous.

In addition, they have had personal experiences that would seem to argue against the dreadful possibility. The actor has played before enthusiastic German audiences. Could these lovers of good theatre possibly sanction such outrages? The waiter, for his part, has served these very inquisitors at the cafe next door, and found them tolerable customers. And surely, one's own special customers cannot be cold-blooded murderers.

Even the more clear-sighted prince seems to have avoided thinking of his cousin as a Nazi, even though he has no use for the group as a whole. And add to this the fact of the merchant's acquired pass, the presence of the non-Jewish prince and gypsy, and hopes keep somehow alive. And if it is pitiable to see these poor doomed individuals delude themselves, there is also the playwright's dire warning that such monstrous acts may again occur unless good men are alert when grave evils threaten.

4. In *Incident at Vichy*, certain common objects are mentioned to dramatize the strange, unnatural way in which the ten men have been snatched from almost painfully ordinary lives. Indicate several that are so used, and show what they are made to signify.

ANSWER: A most striking episode toward the end of the play occurs when the bundle of the aged Jew is ripped open to reveal masses of feathers. The makings of a poor man's one prized pillow or comforter, these scattered feathers point up the pathetic helplessness of the old and feeble who are cruelly jostled off to death.

The order of coffee, brought by the cafe proprietor to the professor and his staff, suggests the simple creature comforts denied the half-fainting artist and the other worried captives. And the waiter's eager reminder that a croissant bun should be ordered for the major calls attention to the fact that very recently he was only the efficient cafe employee serving an agreeable German patron.

The gypsy's pot brings up the whole question of that worthy's occasional thefts. Yet his crimes, however lamented by the merchant, are small as compared with the outrages perpetrated against an entire people. And when the electrician snatches the handle to use it as a possible escape tool, the humble object is used to reveal the ingenuity of the more active, resourceful victims. Other items mentioned are the brass bed and chinaware of the artist's mother, the gold wedding ring held by the boy, and the codeine sought for the toothache of the doctor's wife. All suggest the humdrum lives of average people, and make even more poignant the savage disruptions brought about by the Nazi persecutions.

BIBLIOGRAPHY

PLAYS BY ARTHUR MILLER

After the Fall. New York: Bantam Books, 1965. (Paperback)

All My Sons, in *Six Great Modern Plays.* New York: Dell, 1956. (Paperback) Also in *Collected Plays.*

Collected Plays. New York: The Viking Press, 1958. (Includes *All My Sons, Death of a Saleman, The Crucible, A Memory of Two Mondays,* and *A View from the Bridge.* Also a long, detailed, and helpful Introduction by the playwright.)

Crucible, The. New York: The Viking Press, 1953; Also New York: Bantam Books, 1963. (Paperback) And in *Collected Plays.*

Death of a Salesman. New York: The Viking Press, 1964. (Paperback) Also in *Collected Plays.*

Enemy of the People, An. Adapted from Ibsen. New York: The Viking Press, 1951.

Incident at Vichy. New York: The Viking Press, 1965. (Paperback)

The Man Who Had All the Luck, in *Cross-Section,* ed. E. Seaver. New York: A. A. Wyn, Inc., 1944.

A Memory of Two Mondays, in *Collected Plays;* and with *A View from the Bridge.* New York: The Viking Press, 1955.

A View from the Bridge, in *Collected Plays;* also, The Viking Press, 1955, and by Bantam Books. (Paperbacks)

BOOKS WITH BIOGRAPHICAL AND CRITICAL MATERIAL

Bentley, Eric. *In Search of Theatre.* New York: Alfred A. Knopf, 1953. (Comments on *All My Sons,* pp. 32-33, and on *Death of a Salesman,* pp. 84-87.)

Gassner, John. *The Theatre in Our Times.* New York: Crown Publishers, Inc., 1955 (See *New American Playwrights: Williams, Miller, and Others,* pp. 342-354, and *Death of a Salesman; First Impressions,* 1949, pp. 364-373.)

Heiney, Donald. *Recent American Literature.* New York: Barron's Educational Series, 1958. (Brief biography and studies of principal plays, pp. 400-406.)

Krutch, Joseph Wood. *American Drama since 1918.* New York: G. Braziller, 1957.

Krutch, Joseph Wood. *"Modernism"* in *Modern Drama.* Ithaca, New York: Cornell University Press, 1953. (Comments on *Death of a Salesman.*)

Lewis, Allan. *American Plays and Playwrights of the Contemporary Theatre.* New York: Crown Publishers, Inc., 1965. (Includes comments on *After the Fall* and *Incident at Vichy* in *Arthur Miller, Return to the Self,* pp. 35-52.)

Welland, Dennis. *Arthur Miller.* New York: Grove Press, Inc., 1961. (Paperback. Includes biography and comment on *Focus, The Misfits,* and other works, as well as the plays.)

CRITICAL MATERIAL IN PERIODICALS

Downer, Alan S. "Mr. Williams and Mr. Miller," *Furioso* (Summer, 1949), pp. 66-70.

Driver, Tom F. "Strength and Weakness in Arthur Miller," *Tulane Drama Review,* IV (May, 1960), 45-52.

Gassner, John. "Tragic Perspectives: A Sequence of Queries," *Tulane Drama Review,* II (May, 1958), 7-22. (Comment on *Death of a Salesman,* also reprinted in Hurrell, *Two Modern American Tragedies.*)

Hurrell, John D., ed. Reviews and criticisms of *Death of a Salesman* from various publications by Atkinson, George Jean Nathan, and others, in *Two Modern American Tragedies.* New York: Charles Scribner's Sons, 1961. (Paperback)

Kernodle, George. "The Death of the Little Man," *Tulane Drama Review,* I (1955-6), 47-60. (Comment on *Death of a Salesman.*)

Miller, Arthur. "Tragedy and the Common Man," *New York Times* (Feb. 27, 1949), Sec. 2, pp. 1,3. (Also in Hurrell, *Two Modern American Tragedies.*)

Miller, Arthur, Richard Watts, John Beaufort, *et al.* "A Matter of Hopelessness in *Death of a Salesman. A symposium,"* *Tulane Drama Review,* II (May, 1958), 63-69. (Also in Hurrell, *Two Modern American Tragedies.*)

Tynan, Kenneth. "American Blues. The Plays of Arthur Miller and Tennessee Williams," *Encounter,* II (May, 1954), 13-19. (Also in Hurrell, *Two Modern American Tragedies.*)